Language Disorders in Children and Adolescents

About the Authors

Dr. Joseph H. Beitchman is a clinician and therapist who has been working with children and adolescents with language delays for more than 30 years. He has written extensively on language impairment and its relation to psychiatric disorders, including learning disabilities, anxiety disorders, and disruptive behavior disorders. He is Professor of Psychiatry at the University of Toronto where he teaches and conducts his research.

Dr. Elizabeth Brownlie is a developmental psychologist who works in the area of child, youth, and emerging adult development. Her research focuses on the role of gender, language/learning, and other determinants of health on mental health and wellbeing. She is an Assistant Professor of Psychiatry at the University of Toronto.

Dr. Beitchman and Dr. Brownlie would like to thank Shelly-Anne Li and Lin Bao for their assistance in the preparation of this volume.

Advances in Psychotherapy – Evidence-Based Practice

Series Editor
Danny Wedding, PhD, MPH, Professor of Psychology, California School of Professional
Psychology / Alliant International University, San Francisco, CA

Associate Editors
Larry Beutler, PhD, Professor, Palo Alto University / Pacific Graduate School of Psychology,
Palo Alto, CA
Kenneth E. Freedland, PhD, Professor of Psychiatry and Psychology, Washington University
School of Medicine, St. Louis, MO
Linda C. Sobell, PhD, ABPP, Professor, Center for Psychological Studies, Nova Southeastern
University, Ft. Lauderdale, FL
David A. Wolfe, PhD, RBC Chair in Children's Mental Health, Centre for Addiction and Mental
Health, University of Toronto, ON

The basic objective of this series is to provide therapists with practical, evidence-based treatment guidance for the most common disorders seen in clinical practice – and to do so in a "reader-friendly" manner. Each book in the series is both a compact "how-to" reference on a particular disorder for use by professional clinicians in their daily work, as well as an ideal educational resource for students and for practice-oriented continuing education.

The most important feature of the books is that they are practical and "reader-friendly:" All are structured similarly and all provide a compact and easy-to-follow guide to all aspects that are relevant in real-life practice. Tables, boxed clinical "pearls," marginal notes, and summary boxes assist orientation, while checklists provide tools for use in daily practice.

Language Disorders in Children and Adolescents

Joseph H. Beitchman
Division of Child and Adolescent Psychiatry, University of Toronto, ON, Canada

Elizabeth Brownlie
Centre for Addiction and Mental Health, Toronto, ON, Canada

Library of Congress Cataloging in Publication

is available via the Library of Congress Marc Database under the
Library of Congress Control Number 2012953066

Library and Archives Canada Cataloguing in Publication

Beitchman, Joseph H.
    Language disorders in children and adolescents / Joseph H. Beitchman,
Elizabeth Brownlie.

(Advances in psychotherapy-evidence based practice series ; 28)
Includes bibliographical references.
ISBN 978-0-88937-338-9

    1. Language disorders in children. 2. Language disorders in adolescence.
I. Brownlie, Elizabeth, 1967- II. Title. III. Series: Advances in psychotherapy--
evidence-based practice ; v. 28

RJ496.L35B45 2013   618.92'855   C2012-907447-0

PUBLISHING OFFICES
USA: Hogrefe Publishing Corporation, 38 Chauncy Street, Suite 1002, Boston, MA 02111
                Phone (866) 823-4726, Fax (617) 354-6875; E-mail customerservice@hogrefe-publishing.com
EUROPE: Hogrefe Publishing, Merkelstr. 3, 37085 Göttingen, Germany
                Phone +49 551 99950-0, Fax +49 551 99950-425, E-mail publishing@hogrefe.com

SALES & DISTRIBUTION
USA: Hogrefe Publishing, Customer Services Department,
                30 Amberwood Parkway, Ashland, OH 44805
                Phone (800) 228-3749, Fax (419) 281-6883, E-mail customerservice@hogrefe.com
EUROPE: Hogrefe Publishing, Merkelstr. 3, 37085 Göttingen, Germany
                Phone +49 551 99950-0, Fax +49 551 99950-425, E-mail publishing@hogrefe.com

OTHER OFFICES
CANADA: Hogrefe Publishing, 660 Eglinton Ave. East, Suite 119-514, Toronto, Ontario, M4G 2K2
SWITZERLAND: Hogrefe Publishing, Länggass-Strasse 76, CH-3000 Bern 9

Hogrefe Publishing
Incorporated and registered in the Commonwealth of Massachusetts, USA, and in Göttingen, Lower Saxony,
Germany

Printed and bound in the USA
ISBN: 978-0-88937-338-9

Table of Contents

1

Description

Language impairment (LI) is one of the most common developmental disabilities of childhood. It is especially common among children with emotional or behavior concerns; prevalence is as high as 50% in mental health clinics for children and adolescents (Cohen et al., 1998). The Ottawa Language Study was one of the first longitudinal studies to trace the long term outcomes in a sample of children with speech and/or language impairments (Beitchman, Nair, Clegg, Ferguson & Patel, 1986). The children with speech/language impairment were identified through a screening and assessment process from a random community sample of five-year-old children, thus they were not children who had necessarily come to the attention of clinicians. Contrary to common beliefs when the study commenced in 1985, children with LI persisting to age 5 often do not "grow out of" their language difficulties. What was also unknown at that time was the extent to which children and youth with language difficulties also were dealing with emotional or behavior problems; 42% of children identified with LI at age 5 met criteria for a psychiatric disorder at age 12 (Beitchman, Brownlie, Inglis, Wild, Ferguson et al., 1996).

As has become clear in the years since the study began, language disorders and emotional/behavior problems overlap substantially. This volume is intended to give clinicians working with children and youth insight into how LI may be affecting their clients' lives and suggestions for how to work with and support young people with language difficulties and their families.

1.1   Terminology

Language impairment includes a range of related, often-overlapping difficulties with language expression and/or comprehension. However, terminology to describe language difficulties is not straightforward. Not only are different terms and definitions used in different countries, disciplines, and for clinical versus research applications, terminology is often inconsistent even within these contexts (Bishop, 1997; Kamhi, 1998).

In this volume we focus on *language* impairment more than impairment related to phonology (speech). However, we briefly discuss phonological difficulties as they co-occur with language disorders. The volume addresses language impairment that emerges in childhood, not secondary to a neurological event such as a stroke (i.e., acquired language disorders).

1.1.1　Terms for Language Difficulties

A number of terms have been used to describe language difficulties emerging in childhood, with somewhat different definitions. These include *language impairment, primary language impairment,* and *specific language impairment,* among others. The terms *developmental language impairment / developmental language disorder* are used in some contexts to refer to language impairment emerging in childhood, distinguished from acquired language impairment. *Primary language impairment / primary language disorder* refer to language difficulties that are not primarily attributed to conditions such as developmental delay or hearing impairment. *Specific language impairment* is similar to primary language impairment, but has the additional criterion that language functioning be substantially poorer than nonverbal functioning.

In this text we use *language impairment* (LI) to represent the broad category of *language impairment / language disorder or language delay* – in each case, emerging developmentally. We use LI to describe individuals with language impairment, notwithstanding that they may or may not meet the criteria for a diagnosis according to a given set of criteria at a particular point in time. We use the term *language disorder* when discussing specific diagnoses. As we will describe in more detail, language impairment persists; however, its manifestations shift over development (Conti-Ramsden & Botting, 1999). For the clinician, thinking of language impairment broadly will avoid overlooking clients who may have significant communication difficulties that need to be taken into account for effective treatment.

1.1.2　Diagnostic Criteria for Language Disorders

The *Diagnostic and Statistical Manual of Mental Disorders*, 5th Edition (DSM-5; American Psychiatric Association, 2013) and *International Statistical Classification of Diseases and Related Health Problems,* 10th Edition (ICD-10; World Health Organization, 1992) diagnostic criteria for language disorders are shown in Tables 1 and 2, respectively. Diagnostic subtypes of language disorders in the ICD-10 criteria differentiate between expressive language impairment (difficulties producing language, without impaired comprehension) and receptive language impairment (difficulties comprehending language). Similar subtypes were used in the DSM IV-TR (American Psychiatric Association, 2000), however, the single category language disorder is used in DSM-5.

The ICD-10 includes two mutually exclusive language disorders: expressive language disorder and receptive language disorder. In addition to low (-2 SD) expressive language standardized test scores, the expressive language disorder diagnosis requires that expressive language test scores be at least 1 SD lower than receptive language test scores. The ICD-10 criteria for receptive language disorder do not require poorer receptive language scores than expressive language scores, and in fact do not refer to expressive language performance – thus, an individual with poor scores in both domains could receive the diagnosis of receptive language disorder. This is based on the rationale that expressive language competence requires receptive language competence.

Table 1
Diagnostic Criteria for Language Disorder: DSM-5

	DSM-5 Language Disorder (315.39)
Symptoms	Persistent difficulties in the acquisition and use of language across modalities (i.e., spoken, written, sign language, or other) due to deficits in comprehension or production that include: 1. Reduced vocabulary (word knowledge and use) 2. Limited sentence structure (ability to put words and word endings together to form sentences based on the rules of grammar and morphology 3. Impairments in discourse (ability to use vocabulary and connect sentences to explain or describe a topic or series of events or have a conversation). Language abilities are substantially and quantifiably below those expected for age.
Discrepancy	n/a
Impairment	[Language abilities are substantially and quantifiably below those expected for age,] resulting in functional limitations in effective communication, social participation, academic achievement, or occupational performance, individually or in any combination.
Onset	Onset of symptoms is in the early developmental period.
Exclusions	The difficulties are not attributable to hearing or other sensory impairment, motor dysfunction, or another medical or neurological condition and is not better explained by intellectual disability (intellectual developmental disorder) or global developmental delay.

Reprinted with permission from the *Diagnostic and Statistical Manual of Mental Disorders, Fifth Edition,*© 2013, American Psychiatric Association. All rights reserved.

Table 2
Diagnostic Criteria for Expressive and Receptive Language Disorder: ICD-10

	ICD-10 Expressive Language Disorder (F80.1)	ICD-10 Receptive Language Disorder (F80.2)
Symptoms	Expressive language skills, as assessed on standardized tests, below the 2 standard deviation limit for the child's age.	Receptive language skills, as assessed on standardized tests, below the 2 standard deviation limit for the child's age.
Discrepancy	Receptive language standardized test scores within 2 standard deviations of the mean for the child's age.	Receptive language skills at least 1 standard deviation below nonverbal IQ as assessed on a standardized test.

Table 2 (continued)

	Expressive language standardized test scores at least 1 standard deviation lower than nonverbal IQ.	Use and understanding of non-verbal communication and imaginative language functions within the normal range.
Impairment	n/a	n/a
Onset	n/a	n/a
Exclusions	Absence of neurological, sensory or physical impairments that directly affect use of spoken language, or of a pervasive developmental disorder.	
	Most commonly used exclusion criterion: nonverbal IQ below 70 on a standardized test.	

Reprinted with permission from
WHO. (1992). *The ICD-10 classification of mental and behavioural disorders: Clinical descriptions and diagnostic guidelines.* Geneva: Author. © 1992 World Health Organization.
WHO. (1993). *The ICD-10 classification of mental and behavioural disorders: Diagnostic criteria for research.* Geneva: Author. © 1993 World Health Organization.

The severity of difficulties in the ICD-10 criteria is specified as 2 SD below the mean for age. In addition, a 1 SD discrepancy is needed, with nonverbal IQ at least 1 SD higher than language test scores for the diagnosis to apply. The ICD-10 language disorder diagnoses do not include impairment criteria or onset criteria (although the diagnoses apply to developmental rather than acquired language impairment). Exclusions listed are similar to exclusions for the DSM-5 diagnosis of language disorder.

A new category in DSM-5 is social (pragmatic) communication disorder, which involves difficulties with pragmatics (i.e., social aspects of communication), see Table 3. There is no comparable ICD-10 diagnosis. Pragmatics are particularly relevant to clinicians addressing psychosocial issues because of the overlap between social and communication skills. The DSM-5 social (pragmatic) communication disorder diagnosis is defined by pragmatics difficulties – both expressive, such as difficulties using adaptive language to fit varying social contexts, and receptive, such as difficulties comprehending nuances and social meanings in the communication of others. As with the DSM-5 language disorder diagnosis, onset must be early in development. Impairment in communication, social participation, relationships or academic/occupational functioning is also required. Since pragmatics difficulties are defined by social communication difficulties, impairment is more likely to be noticeable for pragmatics difficulties than for structural language difficulties (i.e., difficulties with vocabulary and grammar that define the language disorders discussed above).

Table 3
Diagnostic Criteria for Social (Pragmatic) Communication Disorder: DSM-5

	DSM-5 Social (Pragmatic) Communication Disorder (315.39)
Symptoms	Persistent difficulties in the social use of verbal and nonverbal communication as manifested by all of the following: 1. Deficits in using communication for social purposes, such as greeting and sharing information in a manner that is appropriate for the social context. 2. Impairment of the ability to change communication to match context or the needs of the listener, such as speaking differently in a classroom than on a playground, talking differently to a child than to an adult, and avoiding use of overly formal language. 3. Difficulties following rules for conversation and storytelling, such as taking turns in conversation, rephrasing when misunderstood, and knowing how to use verbal and nonverbal signals to regulate interaction. 4. Difficulties understanding what is not explicitly stated (e.g., making inferences) and nonliteral or ambiguous meanings of language, for example, idioms, humor, metaphors and multiple meanings that depend on the context for interpretation.
Discrepancy	n/a
Impairment	The deficits result in functional limitations in effective communication, social participation, social relationships, academic achievement, or occupational performance, individually or in combination.
Onset	The onset of the symptoms is in the early developmental period (but deficits may not become fully manifest until social communication demands exceed limited capacities).
Exclusions	The symptoms are not attributable to another medical or neurological condition or to low abilities in the domains of word structure and grammar, and are not better explained by autism spectrum disorder, intellectual disability (intellectual developmental disorder), global developmental delay, or another mental disorder.

1.1.3 Alternative Classification Frameworks for Language Impairment

In addition to the diagnostic schemes in the ICD-10, other subtyping systems exist. For example, Rapin and Allen (1987) described six subtypes of language disorders, with combinations of problems across components of language; other typologies and combinations of difficulties have been proposed (Rapin

& Dunn, 2003). These frameworks point to combinations of communication deficits and strengths that have been observed clinically. However, frameworks proposed to date have limited empirical validation and do not fit the language profile of all children. In addition, profiles of specific language skills shift over time and are not stable across development (Conti-Ramsden & Botting, 1999; Tomblin, Zhang, Buckwalter, & O'Brien, 2003; van Balkom, van Daal, & Verhoeven, 2004).

1.1.4   Speech Disorders

Phonological (speech) impairment often co-occurs with language impairment (Beitchman et al., 1986). Phonological impairment can be expressive (difficulties accurately articulating speech sounds) or receptive (difficulties with speech perception). Phonological errors are developmentally normative in early childhood; when difficulties are persistent and substantially below developmental expectations, phonological disorder diagnoses may apply. These include the DSM-5 speech sound disorder (315.39) and the ICD-10 specific speech phonological disorder (F80.0). The ICD-10 diagnosis of specific speech phonological diagnosis is mutually exclusive with expressive and receptive language disorders; individuals with comorbid speech and language impairment could potentially meet criteria for the ICD-10 diagnosis of either receptive language disorder or expressive language disorder. In contrast, the DSM-5 phonological disorder diagnosis (315.39) does not exclude language disorder; individuals with comorbid speech and language impairment could potentially meet criteria for both language disorder and phonological disorder. Diagnostic criteria for both DSM-5 and ICD-10 phonological disorder exclude difficulties attributable to sensory, physical or neurological impairments. Stuttering [DSM-5 childhood-onset fluency disorder (315.35) or ICD-10 stuttering (F98.5)] is another common speech disorder of children and youth. Unlike phonological disorders, stuttering does not appear to be associated with language impairment (Nippold, 2012).

1.1.5   Historical Terms

Historical terms for language disorders have included: *developmental aphasia* (expressive type; receptive type), *developmental Wernicke's aphasia*, and *developmental dysphasia.* The term *aphasia* is no longer in use because it suggests an impairment that is sudden and acquired through brain damage, which does not apply to developmental language disorders (Bishop, 1997). Historical terms for social (pragmatic) communication disorder are pragmatic language impairment and semantic pragmatic disorder. Historical terms for phonological disorder have included *functional speech articulation disorder, speech articulation developmental disorder,* and *dyslalia* (pronunciation errors); terms specifying particular pronunciation errors have included *lisping* (substituting *th* for *s*) and *lalling* (substituting *w* for *r*). Stuttering has been termed *fluency disorder.*

1.2   Definition

1.2.1   Language Domains

Language use involves multiple skills within a number of domains; these skills involve both receptive (comprehension) and expressive (production) components. Table 4 lists the domains of language and related receptive and expressive skills, under the broad categories of *content, form,* and *use* (Bloom & Lahey, 1978).

Semantics

Semantics, the *content* of language, refers to the meanings of words, phrases, sentences, and discourse more broadly. Receptive semantic skills include receptive vocabulary (knowledge of word meanings) and comprehension of spoken (and written) language; expressive semantic skills include expressive vocabulary (words used in spontaneous speech) and production of utterances that express the intended meaning.

Phonology

The *form* of language includes phonology (speech sounds) and grammar. Receptive phonology includes the perception, recognition, and classification of speech sounds; expressive phonology involves production of speech sounds. Phonological awareness, a related set of skills, includes the ability to parse words into component speech sounds, and to identify and generate rhymes.

Grammar: Morphology and Syntax

Grammar involves both word-level grammatical markers *(morphology)*, for example, the suffix *ed* to indicate past tense; and sentence-level word order rules *(syntax)*, for example, subject – verb – object. Receptive grammar skills involve correct word and sentence interpretation (e.g., for the sentence "The dog will sit behind the cat," understanding the relative positions of the animals and the future timeline). Expressive grammar skills involve the use of morphology and syntax to correctly express precise meaning according to the rules of the particular language.

Pragmatics

Finally, the social use of language is the domain of *pragmatics*. Pragmatics are culturally specific practices and skills related to social uses of language, conversational norms, and the use of nonverbal communication, such as eye contact and gestures. Because *pragmatics* refers to appropriate and/or effective use of language, what constitutes pragmatic difficulties will vary by culture and by social contexts and subcultures. Pragmatics also include skills in social discourse and narrative, such as tailoring speech to the listener, giving appropriate context based on the listener's knowledge, and shaping language to suit particular purposes (e.g., persuasion, apology). Pragmatic skills overlap with social skills and other clinical issues such as social anxiety. In fact, often clinicians work with clients who may not have particular language difficulties, on more effective communication, including aspects of pragmatics.

Table 4
Language Domains

Domain	Component	Definition	Examples of skills and indicators	
			Expressive	Receptive
Content	Semantics	Meaning of words, phrases, sentences, discourse.	Vocabulary used in spontaneous speech *Says "duck."*	Comprehension of words *Can point to a duck.*
				Comprehension of sentences and longer discourse *Understands "The biggest duck quacked the loudest."*
Form	Grammar			
	Syntax	Sentence word order	Sentence complexity and accuracy *Says "I already put my sandwich on the table."*	Correct interpretation of word order *Understands "The duck that was behind the goose swam around the island."*
	Morphology	Grammatical markers (e.g., walked; walks)	Correct usage *Says "I walked."*	Correct interpretation Ability to detect errors
	Phonology	Speech sounds	Production of developmentally appropriate sounds *Pronounces "I thought I saw a rabbit."*	Perception, differentiation, and classification of speech sounds
			Phonological awareness *Produces rhyming words Segments words into speech sounds*	Phonological awareness *Perceive rhymes and speech sounds*
Use	Pragmatics	Social use of speech	Using language effectively for specific purposes	Understand social uses of language, e.g., persuasion, sarcasm
			Conversational skills	

1.2.2 Late Language Emergence

Late language emergence (LLE) refers to early language development that occurs later than expected based on the child's age. Children with LLE have also been described as "late talkers" (e.g., Rescorla, 2005; Whitehouse, Robinson, & Zubrick, 2011) or as having delayed expressive language development. There is considerable variation in the timing of language acquisition and development (Fenson et al., 1994). Children with LLE reach language acquisition milestones (e.g., single words, two-word phrases) substantially later than other children.

Some researchers define LLE by developmental milestones, for example, vocabulary of 50 words and combining words into two- to three-word phrases by 24 months. Children who fail to meet one or both of these milestones constitute the lowest 10%, based on a population sample (Fenson et al., 1993). In other studies, norm-referenced criteria to define LLE are used, such as the 10th percentile or lower score on language acquisition measures or language developmental indices (e.g., Zubrick, Taylor, Rice, & Slegers, 2007). Using this definition, differences from typical development are large; in one study, young children who met criteria for LLE had mean vocabularies of 20 words, versus 235 in the typically developing comparison group (Zubrick et al., 2007). Timing of language development among typically developing children is faster in girls than boys particular at the low end of the distribution, thus boys are considerably more likely to meet criteria for LLE (Zubrick et al., 2007).

Outcomes of Late Language Emergence

Children with LLE continue to have substantially lower vocabularies, and to have less developed skills in other language areas such as grammar, than children who had typical timing of language acquisition (Roos & Weismer, 2008; Weismer, 2007). Although a large proportion of children with LI have experienced LLE, the reverse is not true – the majority of children classified with LLE go on to develop language within the normal range. However, they tend to score in the lower normal range, during childhood and adolescence persistently scoring lower on average than children with typical timing of language acquisition (Rescorla, 2005, 2009). However, children with LLE, unlike children with LI, do not appear to be at increased risk of longer term emotional or behavioral difficulties (Whitehouse et al., 2011).

The majority of "late talkers" develop language within the low normal range

1.2.3 Diagnostic Criteria: Language Impairment / Language Disorders

Three general points are important to emphasize with respect to diagnostic criteria. First, individuals with language impairment / language disorders are heterogeneous. The same diagnostic labels are used for individuals with different profiles of strengths and weaknesses across language and related domains including working memory, auditory and phonological processing, and nonverbal cognitive skills. These profiles of strengths and weaknesses tend to vary over time and may cross diagnostic thresholds, such that individuals

Language disorders are heterogeneous

meet criteria for a diagnosis at some points and are subclinical at others, while continuing to show general difficulties in the communication domain (Bishop, 1997; Conti-Ramsden & Botting, 1999, 2004).

Subclinical levels of language impairment may be important

Second, although it is useful to have clear definitions of language disorders, particularly for research purposes, communication difficulties that do not meet diagnostic criteria may nevertheless be clinically important. There are a number of varying definitions of language disorders; most are primarily based on cutoffs on standardized tests. Children who test above diagnostic thresholds or do not meet exclusionary criteria according to particular diagnostic criteria may nevertheless have communication difficulties that lead to significant impairment, and/or that make conventional modes of treatment unlikely to be effective without adaptation. Clinicians should continue to consider the role that communication difficulties may be playing in a client's life if an assessment identifies subclinical weaknesses in language or other communication domains, even if full criteria for a language disorder are not met.

Language disorders are often unrecognized

Finally, language disorders are often unrecognized. A number of studies have shown that in clinical settings, one third to one half of children may meet criteria for a language disorder, and of these, as many as half may not have been previously diagnosed (Cohen, Davine, Horodezky, Lipsett, & Isaacson, 1993; Cohen, et al., 1998). These numbers increase in inpatient mental health treatment settings and clinical settings for youths involved with the justice system (Giddan, Milling, & Campbell, 1996; Warr-Leeper, Wright, & Mack, 1994). Clinicians working with children and youths need to have language and communication difficulties on their radar even if these issues are not mentioned in the referral or presenting information. "Universal precautions" are needed in working with clients, to avoid overestimating expressive and reception language competence and misattributing comprehension or expression limitations.

Language impairment is both delay and disorder

Language impairment is both delay and disorder. It is a delay in that children and youths with LI have characteristics similar to younger children. For example, children with expressive LI have a mean length of utterance (a metric of language development), that is lower than that of age peers, meaning they use shorter, less complex communication. From this perspective, LI can be understood dimensionally as the lower end of the continuum in language functioning. At the same time, some aspects of language in children with LI, such as inconsistent grammar and phonological processing difficulties, are not characteristic of typical language development (Leonard et al., 2003; Rice & Wexler, 1996).

1.2.4   Expressive Language Impairment

Expressive and receptive symptoms associated with language disorders are shown in Table 5. Children with expressive language impairment generally sound considerably younger than their chronological age, using simpler words and shorter, less complex sentences than their typically developing age peers. They make more grammatical errors than other children – for example, using the wrong endings for verbs or nouns. In particular, inconsistent use of grammatical markers (rather than consistent errors) is a key marker of language impairment (Leonard et al., 2003). Children with expressive LI may also have a limited vocabulary and are often slower than their peers in learning new

Table 5
Symptoms of Expressive and Receptive Language Impairment in Children and Adolescents

Expressive language impairment symptoms

General	– Sounds like younger child or youth – Uses simpler words than age peers – Uses shorter sentences than age peers – Uses less complex sentences than age peers – Uses nonspecific words – Avoids situations requiring speech – Can be misattributed to behavioral, attitudinal, or general cognitive problems
Grammar	– Inconsistent use of markers (morphology) – Incorrect verb agreements – Problems with word order (syntax)
Semantics	– Limited vocabulary in expressive language – Unclear, nonspecific statements or statements that do not reflect intended meaning
Pragmatics	– Inappropriate conversational skills / behavior – Difficulty joining groups already engaged in play or conversation
Discourse	– Difficulty organizing narratives – Difficulty expressing ideas

Receptive language impairment symptoms

General	– Comprehension level similar to a younger child or youth – Difficulty understanding complex sentences – May become frustrated or withdrawn due to lack of comprehension – Noncompliance due to lack of comprehension can be misattributed to behavioral or attitudinal problems
Grammar	– Difficulty interpreting complex sentences
Semantics	– Smaller vocabulary than age peers – Difficulty following conversations – Slower to learn new words
Pragmatics	– Misinterpretation of intent – Difficulty making inferences from language
Discourse	– Difficulty comprehending complex discourse

words (Brackenbury & Pye, 2005), however, for some children with expressive LI, semantics may be an area of relative strength. In addition, children and youths with expressive language disorders may have difficulties at higher levels of discourse, in expressing their ideas and organizing narratives (Vallance, Im, & Cohen, 1999).

Compensating for Language Impairment

Children and youths with expressive LI often use compensatory strategies to cope with their expressive language challenges. For instance, they may frequently use nonspecific words because they are unable to produce an appropriate specific term. They may also respond more globally to their language difficulties by speaking little in social situations and avoiding situations requiring speech. This may partly account for links between LI and social withdrawal or shyness (Bedore & Leonard, 1998; Rice & Wexler, 1996; Voci, Beitchman, Brownlie, & Wilson, 2006).

1.2.5　Receptive Language Impairment

Receptive LI is more subtle and difficult to detect than expressive LI. A child with receptive language difficulties may have difficulties following directions or interpreting situations because of their difficulties with comprehension. It may not be obvious that some of their comprehension difficulties are specifically linguistic (i.e., difficulty processing words or sentences). They may appear to be noncompliant or to have behavioral challenges if they respond inappropriately to verbal requests or other communication. Comorbidity between receptive language impairment and expressive language impairment is expected. This is reflected in the ICD-10 (and DSM-IV-TR) criteria, which include a category for impaired expressive language with unimpaired receptive language, but no category for impaired receptive language with unimpaired expressive language.

Although there are differences between LI children and their typically developing peers, it is important to emphasize that language impairment is subtle, and often undetected. Because language occurs within a specific context, the content of children's communication tends to be noticed and responded to, rather than their language skills and usage, especially for school-aged children. Research shows that adults view children with language impairment more negatively than typically developing children on dimensions outside of the language domain – for example, intelligence, social maturity, leadership potential, and school readiness – on the basis of very brief language samples (Becker, Place, Tenzer, & Frueh, 1991; DeThorne & Watkins, 2001; Rice, Hadley, & Alexander, 1993). It is likely that in situations when language is not made salient, these attributions may overshadow the subtler aspects of communicative competence.

1.2.6　Definitional Issues

Defining language disorders is not straightforward. Different definitions are used for the DSM and ICD (and in their different editions). In research contexts, different criteria are often used for different studies. We discuss a number of definitional issues below.

Clinical Versus Research Contexts

Language disorders are defined relatively stringently in many research studies, as reduced heterogeneity of the sample is helpful to understand causes and outcomes of the disorders (e.g., Bishop, 1997). However, broader definitions make more sense clinically; services are often just as much indicated for children whose difficulties do not correspond to specific diagnostic criteria. In particular, the use of exclusionary criteria may disqualify children who are functioning more poorly and have fewer compensatory skills.

Dimensional Measurement

The ICD-10 language disorders are defined using 2 SD cut-offs on standardized, individually administered language tests. The DSM-5 diagnostic criteria for language disorder require that language skills be quantifiably below age level without specifying a cutoff. Even when cutoffs are specified, the boundaries between LI and meeting criteria for a language disorder are dimensional; the differences between a child scoring at 1.9 versus 2.0 SD below the mean are likely not substantive. In addition, further specific details – for example, how to interpret and integrate results from multiple measures or measures of particular aspects of language – are not specified in DSM-5 or ICD-10 diagnoses. The descriptions of vocabulary, grammar and discourse difficulties with related impairment defining DSM-5 language disorder correspond to the broader clinical assessments typically used by speech/language pathologists (Paul & Norbury, 2012).

Discrepancy Definitions

Definitions of language impairment/disorders typically include a discrepancy between language proficiency and expected proficiency based on (1) other traits such as IQ, or (2) other conditions that may account for lower skill levels, such as developmental delay / mental retardation or autism. Unlike DSM-5, both ICD-10 and DSM-IV-TR use *cognitive referencing*, i.e. defining language disorder as poorer language skills than expected in relation to nonverbal IQ. ICD-10 requires a 1-SD discrepancy between nonverbal IQ and language test scores. In research contexts, specific language impairment has been defined by a discrepancy between language test performance and performance on nonverbal tests; scoring within the normal range on nonverbal IQ is an alternative discrepancy criteria.

Discrepancy definitions have utility for research purposes. They can be used to define a homogeneous sample and to allow focus on differential development in verbal versus nonverbal domains. However, the clinical significance of these discrepancies may be quite different. The discrepancy approach to diagnosis has been the source of ongoing debate among researchers and educators in the field of learning disabilities more broadly.

First, questions have been raised about the validity of assessments since language difficulties may compromise the validity of nonverbal IQ measures. It is not clear the extent to which nonverbal assessment can be wholly independent of verbal ability, since instructions for tasks may not be fully compre-

Problems Using Discrepancy Definitions to Define LI

- Nonverbal assessments may be inaccurate due to verbal aspects of task demands
- Nonverbal IQ not clinically relevant
- Excludes children with greater impairment
- May present an eligibility barrier to children most in need of services

hended. Second, questions have been raised about the relevance of nonverbal IQ, which is not strongly related to language learning and does not affect the impact that language intervention is likely to have (Fey et al., 1994). Third, the impact of higher nonverbal IQ among individuals with LI is a mitigating rather than an exacerbating one. Cognitive strengths in nonverbal domains are associated with more positive outcomes. Children with lower nonverbal IQ are less able to compensate for their verbal difficulties and tend to do more poorly; these children are particularly in need of clinical intervention. Finally, an IQ discrepancy criterion may present a barrier to access to services for youths with greater need for intervention. There is evidence that calculation of IQ–performance discrepancies results in overidentification of children with high IQ and underidentification of children with low IQ. This is an equity issue in that social disadvantage is associated with lower scores on IQ tests (Breslau, Dickens, Flynn, Peterson, & Lucia, 2007).

To summarize, although terminology for language difficulties varies depending on level of nonverbal cognitive functioning or the presence of comorbid conditions, the impact of communication difficulties may be similar across these distinctions. The difficulties a child, adolescent, or adult may experience related to LI are not mitigated based on these conditions – quite the opposite is often true. Children with LI who have strong nonverbal skills tend to have better psychosocial outcomes than children who are poor in nonverbal skills as well. Conversely, a child with lower levels of cognitive functioning in multiple domains may nevertheless have difficulty with communication and comprehension. Therefore it is important for clinicians to be sensitive to possible communication difficulties, especially impaired comprehension, which can easily be overlooked when other issues are present.

1.2.7   Stigma, Labeling, and Terminology

For all mental health and developmental difficulties, stigma is an important issue. Whereas a diagnosis provides important information that can guide intervention and meet eligibility requirements for treatment, diagnostic labels can have negative impacts as well, particularly on the perceptions and expectations based on the diagnosis conferred. Kamhi (1998) notes that there is increased stigma associated with terms such as *disorder* and *impairment,* and that parents of children with LI often do not think of their children in these terms. In addition, stigma can be a barrier that may inhibit parents or youths from seeking services. In contrast, terms such as *language delay* or *language difficulties* may be preferred.

Parents need to understand the difficulties language issues may create for their child

When communicating with parents, it is important to convey the extent to which language issues may be creating difficulties for their child in multiple domains. Terminology can be useful in helping parents understand their child's situation and advocate for services, if needed. Unlike other learning disabilities, language impairment is often unidentified (Cohen et al., 1993). Identifying language issues may decrease other kinds of negative attributions about the child or youth. At the same time, it is important to encourage parents to recognize and build on their child's strengths, especially as his or her social experience with adults and children, and particularly school experiences, may be negative.

1.3   Epidemiology

Law and colleagues (2000) conducted an extensive review of the literature on prevalence of speech and/or LI, based on data from 21 publications reporting on epidemiological studies, generating 16 prevalence estimates. In this review, the median estimate of LI at age 5 was approximately 7% ($M = 6.8\%$, range $= 2\%–10.4\%$). Because of the variations in instruments used to diagnose LI, diagnostic thresholds, and the use of exclusionary criteria, estimates vary considerably. In particular, the use of more stringent cutoffs (e.g., 2 SD below the mean) necessarily results in lower prevalence estimates. Prevalence estimates for subtypes of language disorders are less available and may exclude children with comorbid phonological disorders.

1.3.1   Sex Ratio, Cultural, and Socioeconomic Factors

Reported sex ratios for language disorders are between 1.3:1 and 3:1, boys to girls, based on epidemiological studies. Sex ratios are much more variable in clinical studies. Considerably fewer girls than boys are referred for remediation for speech/language impairment (Zhang & Tomblin, 2000). This may be due in part to the higher rates of comorbid externalizing behavior problems (particularly attention problems and disruptive behavior) that bring boys with LI to the attention of teachers and parents, as well as the generally greater visibility of boys over girls in classrooms (Sadker & Sadker, 1994).

1.4   Course and Prognosis

1.4.1   Early Childhood: Late Language Emergence

Children vary in the age they acquire language. Development of expressive language is more noticeable than receptive language development. Parents may become concerned about children who begin speaking later than other children or whose early expressive language development appears to lag behind that of other children. However, the pace and timing of language development in infancy and early childhood is not very predictive of later language development. In particular, children with late language emergence do not necessarily go on to meet criteria for a language disorder (Roos & Weismer, 2008). In a number of longitudinal studies of following children with LLE, most tested in the normal range in late childhood and adolescence. Their language performance was generally at the low end of the normal range, and lower than typically developing peers (Rescorla, 2009).

However, a subset of children with LLE does go on to meet criteria for language impairment, and late language acquisition is a common feature of LI. Language delays that have not resolved by school entry are associated with longer term difficulties (Law et al., 2000).

Risk for Language Impairment Among Children With Late Language Emergence

Given the variability in outcomes, researchers have attempted to identify which children with LLE should be referred for early intervention. Risk factors for continued LI include family history of speech/language impairment, delays in both receptive and expressive early vocabulary development, and low levels of gestural communication during the preverbal period. Decisions on the need for intervention in late-talking preschool children should take these risk factors, as well as the family/environmental context, into account (Ellis & Thal, 2008).

1.4.2   Child and Adolescent Development

Language impairment can be reliably identified by age 5. Individual profiles across language domains tend to shift across development for children and youths with LI; and children near a diagnostic threshold may fluctuate in whether they meet full diagnostic criteria for a language disorder (Bishop, 1997; Conti-Ramsden & Botting, 1999; Tomblin et al., 2003). Nevertheless, relative performance in language domains is stable; youths with low language performance continue to score low (Beitchman et al., 1994, 2001; Tomblin et al., 2003). Persistence is greatest among children with the most pervasive LIs (Beitchman, Wilson, Brownlie, Walters, & Lancee, 1996; Law et al., 2000; Tomblin et al., 2003). Language intervention can improve language functioning in some domains, especially among children with primarily expressive impairment and stronger receptive language skills (Law, Garrett, & Nye, 2004). However, a large proportion of children and youths continue to have language deficits even if they receive intervention.

Impairment related to LI is common in childhood and adolescence. Reading and other academic difficulties are common (Young et al., 2002). Adjustment difficulties and behavior problems at school can develop secondary to academic problems and problems with peers. Social problems are a continuing challenge for many children and youths with LI and appear closely tied to their communication difficulties. Children with LI may show social withdrawal, have difficulties with social participation, tend to have poorer social skills than peers, and have more difficulties forming friendships (Durkin & Conti-Ramsden, 2010; Fujiki, Brinton, Morgan, & Hart, 1999). Children and youths with LI also tend to be viewed more negatively by peers and are more likely to experience peer victimization (Durkin & Conti-Ramsden, 2010). However, psychosocial outcomes are variable; some youths with LI show good adjustment.

1.4.3   Adult Outcomes

In epidemiological research, about three quarters of children (73%) with age 5 language impairment continued to meet criteria at age 19, based on comprehensive speech/language assessments at baseline and follow-up (Johnson et al., 1999). Definitions of language disorders are based on age-graded standardized measures. The persistence of LI means that most children with LI do not "catch up" to their peers. Although the language skills of children with expressive language disorder or mixed expressive–receptive disorder improve with development, a gap between language test scores of youths with and without a history of childhood language impairment tends to persist into adulthood (Beitchman et al., 2008).

Early clinic-based studies of individuals with relatively severe LI reported significant psychosocial difficulties in adulthood; however, this may reflect referral bias. Data from an epidemiological sample has reported positive psychosocial outcomes for young adults with a history of LI, even though language deficits persisted (Johnson, Beitchman & Brownlie, 2010). Young adults with LI appeared to choose careers with reduced verbal demands. The outcomes for young women with LI were variable, with high rates of early parenting and lower income levels than women without a history of LI. Both women and men with LI reported similarly high quality of life, to controls with typically developing language. Thus, even for individuals with persisting language difficulties, psychosocial impairment may remit for many young people with LI, perhaps due in part to the end of compulsory education and the increase in available life choices.

1.5 Differential Diagnosis

1.5.1 Developmental Delay / Intellectual Disabilities / Mental Retardation

Intellectual disability / developmental delay (nonverbal and verbal IQ below 70) is a common exclusionary criterion for language disorders. Similar to children with LI, children with more global cognitive delays will tend to show LLE and poorer expressive and receptive language than expected for their age, and may have difficulties in language use / pragmatics. Delayed motor development has been reported among children with language disorders; this may be another common characteristic. Psychometric assessment of nonverbal cognitive functioning, will distinguish these two groups. This can be complicated as there are verbal demands in many nonverbal assessments, which can lead to misclassification of children with receptive and expressive language impairments. As has been mentioned, the language intervention needs of children who fall below the IQ cutoff (70) may not be especially different from those of children above the threshold; and low nonverbal IQ is not a barrier to effective language interventions.

1.5.2 Environmental Deprivation

Because of the need for rich linguistic stimulation from infancy for typical language development, environmental deprivation can result in delayed or impaired language. Severe disturbances in language development may provide an alert for the need for intervention in cases of severe neglect. Depending on the severity, children whose LI is secondary to environmental deprivation may or may not show concomitant developmental lags in other

domains. The child's developmental history, if available, indicates if deprivation is present. If LI does arise secondarily to environmental deprivation,
children may show rapid gains after placement in an environment that meets
their needs. However, because of sensitive periods in language development,
children with this history may experience long-term language difficulties and
may require intervention.

1.5.3   Autism Spectrum Disorder / Pervasive Developmental Disorders

Autism spectrum disorder / pervasive developmental disorders are exclusionary criteria for language disorders in both the DSM-5 and ICD-10. Children
in the autism spectrum show significant LI. In addition to rigid, stereotyped
behavior patterns, stereotyped expressive language, avoidance of eye contact,
and problems with social reciprocity are the hallmarks of an autistic spectrum
disorder. In the DSM-5, autism spectrum disorder is defined by the presence
of both impaired social communication and two or more symptoms of rigid /
stereotyped behavior.

Some children with LI, particularly those with pragmatics difficulties, may
show features usually associated with autism, such as problems with social
reciprocity. Ordinarily they would not show the ritualized and stereotyped
behavior typical of children with diagnoses in the autism spectrum, which
tends to provide the strongest basis for differential diagnosis (Barrett, Prior,
& Manjiviona, 2004). In fact, children who would have met criteria for DSM
IV-TR pervasive developmental disorder not otherwise specified, i.e., those
communication deficits and with narrow and possibly unusual interests, who
do not show substantial stereotyped behavior - may meet criteria for DSM-5
social (pragmatic) communication disorder rather than autism spectrum disorder (Taheri & Perry, 2012).

The child with LI primarily in pragmatics, i.e., with social (pragmatic)
communication disorder, previously termed pragmatic language impairment
or semantic–pragmatic disorder, can represent the most challenging differential from a child with autism (Bishop & Norbury, 2002). Children with these
impairments show impaired social reciprocity, and their abnormal symbolic and
imaginative play can be attributed to delayed semantic–pragmatic development.

There is controversy on the degree and meaning of overlap of social and
language difficulties that characterize both sets of disorders. However, both
social and language deficits will need to be addressed in interventions for
children in both populations (e.g., Leyfer, Tager-Flusberg, Dowd, Tomblin, &
Folstein, 2008; Whitehouse, Barry, & Bishop, 2008).

1.5.4   Selective Mutism

The selectively mute child can and does speak at home with family members,
but outside the home is silent, communicating with gestures and facial nods
etc. Although selective mutism is an anxiety disorder, preliminary research
suggests that children with selective mutism may have subtle language and/or

auditory processing deficits; other developmental delays (cognitive and motor) have also been identified (Manassis et al., 2007). As such, selective mutism represents a subset of children with comorbid anxiety and speech and language delays (Beitchman & Inglis, 1991; Manassis et al., 2007).

The assessment of the child's language development can be challenging given that the child may refuse to speak to the assessor. A careful history from the parents can help identify if there are obvious or gross delays in the child's acquisition of language. Additionally, the parents can be asked to tape-record conversations with the child to obtain a sample of the child's expressive language.

1.6   Comorbidities

Common comorbidities with language impairment include phonological disorders, academic/learning disabilities, anxiety disorders, attention deficit disorders, and (to a lesser extent, and specific to males) disruptive behavior (conduct disorder, delinquency, and/or antisocial personality disorder) (Beitchman et al., 2001; Brownlie et al., 2004; Rutter et al., 1997).

1.6.1   Phonological Disorder

In early childhood, delays in the development of speech sounds are common among children with LI. Comorbidity of language disorders and phonological disorders is substantial (Pennington & Bishop, 2009). Because phonological disorders tend to resolve, comorbidity is much reduced by middle childhood. Children with comorbid language and phonological disorders have a significantly increased risk of reading disorders and may have greater severity of LI (Pennington & Bishop, 2009).

1.6.2   Learning Disabilities

Language impairment is associated with academic difficulties. The greatest comorbidity is with reading disorder, possibly due to shared phonological demands (Pennington & Bishop, 2009). However, difficulties in other academic areas including math are common, likely due to the importance of reading, listening, and speaking in most academic work (Young et al., 2002).

1.6.3   Anxiety Disorders

Anxiety disorders are among the most common comorbid conditions of children and youths with LI (Beitchman, Brownlie et al., 1996; Beitchman et al., 2001). Similar overlap between language disorders and internalizing disorders has been reported in both speech/language and mental health clinical settings, with the highest rates of anxiety associated with language (rather than speech) impairment (Redmond & Rice, 1998).

In young children, social withdrawal is common among children with LI; language difficulties should be considered and investigated among young children exhibiting persistent symptoms of withdrawal from peers (Fujiki, Brinton, Morgan, & Hart, 1999). Avoidance or difficulty participating in social interactions can be a consequence of limited comprehension and difficulties with verbal communication, both of which hinder spontaneous social participation. Anxiety related to school may develop in response to academic difficulties and/or peer problems, including victimization and exclusion (Conti-Ramsden & Botting, 2004). As discussed above, selective mutism is an anxiety disorder that affects a subset of children with comorbid language impairment, especially those with high levels of social anxiety (Manassis et al., 2007). Older children and youths with LI may experience social phobia or subclinical social anxiety symptoms, often related to public speaking and/or social interaction (Voci et al., 2006).

1.6.4   Attention-Deficit/Hyperactivity Disorder

Attention-deficit/hyperactivity disorder (ADHD) is highly comorbid with language impairment (Beitchman, Brownlie, et al., 1996; Beitchman, Nair, Clegg, Ferguson, & Patel, 1986; Cohen et al., 2000). The shared features in both sets of difficulties include problems with working memory (greater among children with LI), academic difficulties, problems with self regulation, and verbal mediation of problem behavior. Children with ADHD tend to have difficulties in the language domains of pragmatics and discourse, due to their impulsivity. Social problems can also develop for children with ADHD or LI, possibly associated with difficulties with pragmatics and discourse in both groups. Because of the overlapping areas of deficit, differentiating between ADHD and LI can be challenging. High rates of unidentified language disorders have been found among children with ADHD in clinical populations, as language assessments are often not undertaken, despite the close association between language and ADHD and the language-based aspects of treatment (Cohen et al., 2000).

1.6.5   Conduct Disorders / Delinquency

Language impairment is also somewhat associated with conduct problems in boys (Beitchman et al., 2001). There is a well-documented association between verbal skills and delinquency (Lynam, Moffitt, & Stouthamer-Loeber, 1993; Moffitt, 1993). While not necessarily causative, LI is often a strong contributor to disruptive behavior. Academic and school behavioral difficulties likely account for some of this association. In addition, youths with limited language capacity may experience challenges moderating their impulses and dealing with complex social situations through oral discourse. Boys with LI have an increased risk of arrest by age 19 (Brownlie et al., 2004) and are more likely to meet criteria for antisocial personality disorder (Beitchman et al., 2001). Rates of unidentified LI are high in youth justice and treatment settings (Warr-Leeper et al., 1994). Youths who become involved in the justice system may have a limited ability to understand and participate in the process (Lavigne & Van Rybroek, 2010; Snow & Powell, 2012).

1.6.6   Other Mental Health Concerns

The stress associated with school demands, especially in relatively rigid academic environments that do not accommodate learning difficulties, may be associated with adjustment difficulties; untreated, these may develop into internalizing or disruptive behavior disorders (DBDs). In addition to disorders with known associations with language disorders, LI may co-occur with other disorders that do not have increased prevalence among youths with LI. LI can be a complicating factor in identification and treatment of other disorders. The role of language difficulties and associated functional impairment in other emotional or behavioral issues should also be assessed, and plans should be made to increase support for the child or youth.

1.7   Diagnostic Procedures and Documentation

Diagnosis of language and phonological disorders is often done in collaboration with speech/language pathologists. Diagnostic approaches for communication disorders vary depending on the age of the child. For preschool and school-aged children and adolescents, standardized measures can be used to determine whether the child meets criteria for a language disorder and to profile their strengths and weaknesses. For younger children who are acquiring language, assessment may include measures in which parents report on the child's language development and analysis of language samples recorded at the clinic and/or at home.

1.7.1   Language Screening

Screening procedures identify children and adolescents with possible language disorders; if indicated, assessment by a speech-language pathologist can confirm that a significant problem exists and produce a more detailed language and speech profile to clarify the child's strengths and weaknesses. Given the high degree of overlap between language impairment and emotional/behavioral concerns, children presenting to mental health settings should be considered at high risk of language impairment and should be screened if language issues are not flagged as a presenting concern (Cohen et al., 1998). Table 6 lists some common screening tools for language impairment. Approaches to screening vary according to the age of the child.

0–2 years: Universal hearing screening for newborns is mandated in many jurisdictions. In the absence of screening, infant hearing impairment is often not identified until the child is over 12 months of age (Wolff et al., 2010). This can result in language delay due to decreased language stimulation during a sensitive period. In addition to hearing impairment, a low level of intentional communication (gestures, vocalizations or words) by age 1 signals the need for further assessment (Crais, 2011).

2–3 years: The timing of early language development is variable; although language delay can be identified by age 2 or 3, it is difficult to distinguish those children who will develop LI and those whose late language emergence will resolve into development in the normal range (Conti-Ramsden & Durkin, 2012). However, broader developmental issues (e.g., autism, developmental delay) can often be identified. Developmental screening tools with good psychometric properties are available with subscales tapping communication (i.e., to detect current delay); for a review, see Prelock, Hutchins, and Glascoe (2008).

Although screening before age 3 may not distinguish language impairment from late language emergence, children with delayed language development may nevertheless benefit from early intervention even if their language would have recovered to the normal range without intervention. Expressive vocabulary less than 50 words and/or failure to combine words after age 2 is a commonly-used criterion for language delay (Roos & Weismer, 2008). Particularly for higher risk children, supporting caregivers in providing environments promoting language development may be beneficial not only in strengthening language development but also promoting literacy (e.g., encouraging book reading) and strengthening the parent-child relationship (e.g., teaching parents to follow the child's lead in interactions), all of which may reduce risk for subsequent emotional or behavioral problems.

3–5 years: Identification of language difficulties in the preschool period allows time for intervention before formal schooling begins and reading demands increase. Unfortunately, limitations in quality of psychometric information available and varied definitions of language impairment and populations screened in validation studies, there are no simple recommendations for preschool language screening (Law, Boyle, Harris, Harkness, & Nye, 2000; Nelson, Nygren, Walker & Panoscha, 2006; Eriksson, Westerlund, & Miniscalco, 2010; Conti-Ramsden & Durkin, 2012). Emerging evidence suggests that memory-based screens (sentence repetition and non-word repetition tasks), which are discussed below with respect to school-age children, are showing promise in identifying younger children with LI (Chiat & Roy, 2007; Seeff-Gabriel, Chiat & Roy, 2008).

Approaches to screening young children include parent reports on the child's language skills and/or parental concerns about their language, and direct assessment of the child's communication. Parent reports on standardized checklists and/or expressed parental concern can be as effective as screening the child directly, and may exceed direct assessments in identifying problems with pragmatics (Bishop, 2003; Glascoe, 1997). Some parents of young children referred for clinical services may have challenges, stressors or health issues that compromise their ability to report on their children's language development. On the other hand, some children may not perform well in a formal testing context, or their difficulties with verbal communication may not be evident in a highly structured setting. A combination of direct child assessment and parent-report is a reasonable approach in this age group in clinical settings and can increase accuracy (Bishop and McDonald, 2009).

Comprehensive speech-language assessment is indicated if problems are identified by either screening approach. A multi-informant approach is espe-

Table 6
Examples of Language Screening Tools

Screening Test	Age (years)	Time (minutes)	Domains
Direct child assessment			
Early Repetition Battery (Seeff-Gabriel, Chiat, & Roy, 2008)	2–6	10–15	Phonological memory (marker of language impairment)
Sentence Repetition Screening Test (Sturner, Kunze, Funk, & Green, 1993)	4–5	3	Phonological memory (marker of language impairment); articulation
Children's Test of Nonword Repetition (Gathercole & Baddeley, 1996)	4–8	15	Phonological memory (marker of language impairment)
Clinical Evaluation of Language Fundamentals – Screening Test (Semel, Wiig & Secord, 2004)	5–21	15	Receptive and expressive grammar and semantics
Parent report / parental concerns			
Children's Communication Checklist – 2 (Bishop, 2003).	4–16	5–15	Multiple domains including syntax and semantics; focus on pragmatics
Language Development Survey (Klee et al., 1998; Rescorla, 1987).	1½–3	10	Expressive language
Parents' Evaluation of Developmental Status (Glascoe, 1997)	0–8	3	Parental concern re language development

cially important for children learning multiple languages or who use language dialects that assessors may not be familiar with; parents will be familiar with additional languages or dialects and can therefore provide important contextual information.

School-age children: Sentence repetition tasks, which require children to repeat back sentences with varying length and complexity, are quick to administer and among the most effective at identifying children with language difficulties (Archibald & Joanisse, 2009; Conti-Ramsden, 2003). They are also relatively unbiased to differences in dialect and socioeconomic status, an important strength (Chiat & Roy, 2007). The Children's Test of Non-word Repetition has also been shown to distinguish children with and without language impairment, however, research to date suggests that sentence repetition performs better (Archibald & Gathercole, 2006; Gathercole & Baddeley, 1996). Sentence repetition subscales are available in standardized tests such as the Clinical Evaluation of Language Fundamentals – 4 (CELF-4; Semel, Wiig, & Secord, 2003). Another approach for screening school-age children is to use screens constructed with items selected across language domains from full language assessment tests based on their ability to identify language impairment, such as the Clinical Evaluation of Language Fundamentals-4 Screening Test (Semel, Wiig & Secord, 2004).

Incorporation of Risk Factors in Screening

Language screening should be based on the child's current language functioning; there is no empirical support for screening on the basis of known risk factors, e.g., screening for parental language delay, rather than child language (Nelson et al, 2006). Nonetheless, there may be important ways in which risk factors may play a role in decision-making around language screening. Children with environmental risk factors who have borderline results on language screening may benefit from assessment and early intervention, as these environmental risk factors may be ongoing, with ongoing increased risk (Paul & Norbury, 2012). Because children referred for emotional or behavioral problems are at risk, a full speech/language assessment may be warranted on the basis of parental concern or evidence of language difficulties, even if subthreshold. Although boys are at greater risk of LI than girls, caution should be used in referring boys but not girls who perform similarly on language screens, given that girls with LI have been shown to be less likely to receive intervention than boys with LI (Zhang & Tomblin, 2000).

1.7.2   Language Assessment

When language concerns are identified on referral or after screening, a comprehensive assessment by a speech/language pathologist is important to better understand the client's language profile. General language measures include overall standard scores and typically include scores for receptive and expressive language functioning. In addition, separate subscale scores may be provided by language domain (e.g., semantics). Some tests include subscales for pragmatics, however, many do not; separate pragmatics measures are available, as are many measures addressing more specific aspects of communication. Some commonly used language assessments are shown in Table 7.

In addition to norm-referenced measures that show the extent to which scores deviate from population norms, indicating significant issues, criterion-referenced measures assess specific language skills, which generates a more detailed language profile that identifies targets for intervention. Other approaches that provide contextual information to guide diagnosis and intervention include dynamic assessment, which assesses the ways the client is able to respond to the therapist's intervention, and analysis of language samples of the child's speech either in the lab or, for younger children, at home.

1.7.3   Assessment Tools for Behavioral and Emotional Concerns

A comprehensive assessment of behavioral and emotional concerns will usually be based on information from multiple informants; typically information

Table 7
Common Language Assessments by Language Domain

Test name	Age range	Time (minutes)	Phonology		Semantics		Syntax		Morphology		Pragmatics
			Expressive	Receptive	Expressive	Receptive	Expressive	Receptive	Expressive	Receptive	
Comprehensive Language Assessment											
Comprehensive Assessment of Spoken Language (CASL; Carrow-Woolfolk, 1999a)	3–21	30–45			✓	✓	✓	✓			✓
Clinical Evaluation of Language Fundamentals, 4th ed. (CELF-4; Semel, Wiig, & Secord, 2003)	5–21	30–60	✓	✓	✓	✓	✓	✓			✓
Diagnostic Evaluation of Language Variation (DELV; Seymour, Roeper, & deVilliers, 2005)	4–9	45–50	✓	✓	✓	✓	✓	✓			✓
Oral and Written Language Scales, 2nd ed. (OWLS-2; Carrow-Woolfolk, 2011)	3–21	10–30			✓	✓	✓	✓			✓
Preschool Language Scales, 5th ed. (PLS–5; Zimmerman, Steiner, & Pond, 2011)	Birth–7	45–60			✓	✓	✓	✓	✓	✓	
Test of Early Language Development, 3rd ed. (TELD-3; Hresko, Reid, & Hammill, 1991)	2–7	15–45			✓	✓	✓	✓			

Table 7 (continued)

Test name	Age range	Time (minutes)	Phonology		Semantics		Syntax		Morphology		Pragmatics
			Expressive	Receptive	Expressive	Receptive	Expressive	Receptive	Expressive	Receptive	
Test of Language Development – Primary, 4th ed. (TOLD-P 4; Hammill & Newcomer, 2008b)	4–8	60	✓	✓	✓	✓	✓	✓	✓		
Test of Language Development – Intermediate, 4th ed. (TOLD-I 4; Hammill & Newcomer, 2008a)	8–17	30–60			✓	✓	✓	✓	✓		
Test of Adolescent and Adult Language, 4th ed. (Hammill, Brown, Larsen, & Wiederholt, 2007)	12–24	60–180			✓	✓	✓	✓			
Expressive Language											
Bankson Language Test, 2nd ed. (BLT-2; Bankson, 1990)	3–6	30			✓		✓		✓		✓
Bracken Basic Concept Scale: Expressive, 3rd ed. (BBCS-E; Bracken, 2006)	3–6	20–25			✓						
The Expressive Language Test 2 (Bowers, Huisingh, LoGiudice & Orman, 2010)	5–11	35			✓		✓				✓
Illinois Test of Psycholinguistic Abilities, 3rd ed. (ITPA-3; Hammill, Mather, & Roberts, 2001)	5–2	45–60	✓		✓		✓				

Table 7 (continued)

Test name	Age range	Time (minutes)	Phonology		Semantics		Syntax		Morphology		Pragmatics
			Expressive	Receptive	Expressive	Receptive	Expressive	Receptive	Expressive	Receptive	
Receptive language											
Peabody Picture Vocabulary Test, 4th ed. (PPVT-4; Dunn & Dunn, 2007)	2–90+	10–15				✓					
Boehm Test of Basic Concepts, 3rd ed. (BOEHM-3; Boehm, 2000)	Grade K–2	30–45				✓					
Test for Auditory Comprehension of Language, 3rd ed. (TACL-3; Carrow-Woolfolk, 1999b)	3–9	15–25				✓		✓			
Pragmatics											
Test of Pragmatic Language, 2nd ed. (TOPL-2; Phelps-Terasaki, & Phelps-Gunn, 2007)	6–18	45–60									✓
Pragmatic Language Skills Inventory (PLSI; Gilliam, & Miller, 2006)	5–12	5–10									✓
Pragmatic Language Observation Scale (PLOS; Hammill, & Newcomer, 2009)	8– 7	5–10									✓

is obtained from the child or adolescent, the parents, and the child's teachers. Occasionally, collateral information can be obtained from other sources such as counselors at a summer camp, or a coach or group leader. Information from these latter sources can be helpful if there is continuing uncertainty about the child's behavior, and the child is reported to be behaving differently in these different settings.

To assist the assessment process, there are numerous questionnaires and instruments that will be helpful in describing the child's difficulties; a short list is provide in Table 8. These should not be used in isolation but to inform case formulation. The information from these instruments can also be used to help guide the treatment, and inform the child and parent of the specific areas of difficulty for the child or adolescent.

It is usually helpful to use at least one broad-based questionnaire, such as the Achenbach Child Behavior Checklist, to obtain some quantitative information on the child's behavior across a wide range of symptom categories to assess the degree to which the problems are restricted to certain behaviors and situations versus being more widespread. This information helps guide the approach to treatment. In addition to broad-based questionnaires, questionnaires that directly assess the behaviors or symptom categories of concern should also be administered. In administering self-report instruments, carefully attend to the child's reading level because the questions may exceed the child's reading level and may need to be read to him or her.

The results of these questionnaires should be reviewed with the parent and child or youth, and ambiguities and inconsistencies discussed until a satisfactory understanding is achieved. In planning a cognitive behavior therapy (CBT) approach, documenting the child's or youth's thinking processes provides therapeutic targets and forms a basis for tracking the child's progress in therapy.

Table 8 is a short list of commonly used questionnaires, with the ages for which they are intended and the type of content that is targeted. These questionnaires are intended to assess broad-based behavior and emotional problems, symptoms of anxiety, depression, disruptive behavior symptoms including ADHD symptoms, and cognitive content aimed at negative self-talk.

Table 8
Assessment Measures for Behavioral and Emotional Concerns

Instrument	Age range (years)	Description
Achenbach System of Empirically Based Assessments (ASEBA; Achenbach, 2009)	1.5–90+	Comprehensive. Parent, teacher, and self-reports. Problem behavior and DSM-IV subscales; internalizing, externalizing, and adaptive/competence scales. 20–40 minutes.
Conners Rating Scales – Revised (CRS-R; Conners, 1997)	3–17	ADHD and related problems. Parent, teacher, and adolescent self-reports. Problem behavior and DSM-IV symptom scales. 15–20 minutes; 5–10 minute screens.
Revised Children's Manifest Anxiety Scale, 2nd ed. (RCMAS-2; Reynolds & Richmond, 2008)	6–19	Anxiety symptoms. Self-report. Total score and subscales for types of anxiety, including social anxiety; social desirability (lie) scale. Audio CD administration for children with language or reading difficulties. 10–15 minutes; 5 minute short form.

Table 8 (continued)

Instrument	Age range (years)	Description
Screen for Child Anxiety Related Emotional Disorders – Revised (SCARED-R; Muris, 1997)	8–18	Anxiety symptoms. Self-report; original version has parent-report. Overall and DSM-IV anxiety disorder symptom subscales. 20 minutes.
Children's Depression Inventory 2 (CDI 2; Kovacs, 2010)	7–17	Depressive symptoms. Parent, teacher, and self-reports. Emotional and functional problem scales; four subscales. 15–20 minutes. 5 minute short form.
SNAP-IV (Swanson, 2011)	6–18	ADHD and oppositional defiant disorder DSM-IV symptoms. Parent and teacher reports. ADHD core symptom and oppositional subscales. 10 minutes.
Beck Anger Inventory for Youth (BANI-Y; Beck et al., 2005)	7–18	Anger. Self-report. Scale assesses angry feelings and related cognitions, including attributions of hostile intent. 5–10 minutes.
Children's Inventory of Anger (ChIA; Nelson & Finch, 2000)	6–16	Anger. Self-report. Identifies situations provoking anger and response intensity. 10 minutes.
Children's Automatic Thoughts (CATS; Schniering & Rapee, 2002)	7–16	Negative cognitions about self and others. Self-report. Hostility, physical, social, and failure subscales. 10 minutes.
Negative Affect Self-Statement Questionnaire (NASSQ; Ronan, Kendall, & Rowe, 1994)	7–15	Anxiety- and depression-related thoughts and feelings. Self-report. Items are statements generated by children and adolescents. Anxiety and depression subscales. 5–10 minutes.
The Behavioral and Emotional Rating Scale, 2nd ed. (BERS-2; Epstein, 2004).	5–18	Strengths and competencies. Self-report. Parent and teacher versions available but use self-report scoring. Intra- and inter-personal, affect, school, family, career subscales. 10 minutes.

Note. ADHD = attention-deficit/hyperactivity disorder.

2

Theories and Models of Language Disorders in Children and Adolescents

2.1   Typical Language Development

To understand LI, it is helpful to consider the complexity involved in spoken language. Language comprehension and expression involve multiple skills that develop rapidly over the first years of life. For example, comprehension of a full sentence involves parsing complex sound waves into speech sounds and word segments, and applying knowledge of word meanings and grammar (word order and grammatical markers), all in relation to contextual cues and background knowledge that guide interpretation (Bishop, 1997).

Given the complexity of language production and comprehension, children learn language remarkably quickly. Selected milestones of speech/language development and their typical age are shown in Table 9. Milestones give an indication of expected timing of language acquisition; however, there is considerable variability in the age different aspects of language emerge among typically developing children (Fenson et al., 1993).

2.1.1   Prenatal and Neonatal Development

Language development begins prenatally, as demonstrated by studies with infants shortly after birth. Newborns can discriminate between auditory stimuli they were exposed to prenatally and comparable, novel stimuli; can distinguish between different languages; show a preference for the language they were exposed to in utero; and prefer their mother's voice over another woman's voice, on the first day of life (Decasper & Fifer, 1980; Fava, Hull, & Bortfeld, 2011). Neural studies confirm that language-processing mechanisms, accompanied by *brain lateralization,* exist at birth. In addition, infants' sensory capacities support social interaction, which in turn facilitates language development. For example, infants visually orient to human faces more than to comparable stimuli, which supports their attention to linguistic stimulation. These mechanisms and capacities interact with environmental inputs to facilitate language development, as infants tune their general capacity for language learning to their specific language environments (Fava et al., 2011).

Phonological Development
At birth, infants are able to discriminate between almost all speech sounds used in human languages. Over time, infants' discrimination abilities decrease for sounds that are not included in their language environments. By 6 months

Table 9
Selected Milestones of Speech/Language Development

Age (years)	Phonology	Semantics	Syntax	Pragmatics
0–1	Cooing, progressing into vowel-like sounds	Understands up to 50 words		Orients to faces; pays attention to caregivers' actions
	Babbling (consonant-vowel combinations) emerges, becomes increasingly speech-like	Looks up, turns to source when hearing own name		Vocalizes in response to speech and initiates vocalizations to others
	Perception, production reflect first language's speech sound categories			Uses gestures and vocalizes to request, refuse, comment
				Participates in turn-taking games
1–2	Uses systematic strategies to simplify pronunciation (e.g., only pronouncing stressed syllable of word)	Understands various kinds of two-word phrases	Uses two-word, telegraphic (grammatically unmarked) phrases	Initiates joint attention by pointing or vocalizing
		Uses *no* and *more*	Uses a consistent word order of subject, verb, and noun	Acknowledges others' speech vocally or with eye contact
	At 24 months, half of the speech the child produces is intelligible	Answers yes/no and *what's this?* questions	Refers to self using *me* and own name	Uses words to request, refuse, comment
	Pronounces 70% of consonants correctly	By 24 months, expressive vocabulary of 200 to 300 words		

Table 9 (continued)

Age (years)	Phonology	Semantics	Syntax	Pragmatics
2–3	At 36 months, three quarters of the child's speech is intelligible Continues to use simplifications and sound substitutions Becomes aware of and can produce rhymes	Asks and understands simple questions with *who, what, where* about people, objects and events Asks and understands *why* questions Development of syntax supports semantics learning and vice versa	Understands person pronouns Uses *gonna, wanna* etc.; later begins to use *can, will* Begins to use grammatical markers, e.g., /s/ for plural Over-regularizes past-tense rules (e.g., *runned* instead of *ran*)	Uses words for symbolic play, teasing, dissimulation Talks about objects not currently present Answers some requests for clarification of own speech Responds on topic nearly half the time
3–4	Intelligibility continues to improve A few simplification strategies remain (e.g., consonant blends pronounced as single consonants)	Understands and uses words for color, size, kinship relationships Understands and asks *when* and *how* Uses vocabulary to coin a term when they do not know a word	Expresses possession using 's Produces phrases with 4–5 words, including some complex sentence forms Uses articles, irregular past tense	Uses words to express emotions, retell past events, reason, and for imaginary play Begins to simplify language when speaking to younger children Narratives emerge with theme and some temporal elements

Table 9 (continued)

Age (years)	Phonology	Semantics	Syntax	Pragmatics
4–5	Speech becomes fully intelligible	Starts to understand numbers and counting	Produces longer sentences with more complex grammatical structure	Can express requests indirectly
	Errors on some consonants may persist (particularly s, sh, r, l, v, z, zh, ch and j)	Starts to learn letter names and sounds	Able to use and understand basic sentence forms	Adjusts speech based on social expectations
	Begins to be able to segment words into syllables	Asks for the meaning of new words		Narratives become sequences of events
5–7	Almost all speech errors disappear	Expressive vocabulary size on average 3000-5000 words	Begins to use and understand passive constructions	Narratives use story form with focus, climax, resolution
	Begins to be able to segment words into speech sounds	Receptive vocabulary larger than expressive	Continues to improve ability to produce complex sentences	Extends oral language skills to reading and writing

Adapted from: Berk, L. E. (2000). *Child development* (5th ed.). Boston: Allyn & Bacon. © 2000 A. Pearson Education Company, 160 Gould Street, Needham Heights, MA, 02494; Paul, R., & Norbury, C.F. (2012) *Language disorders from infancy to adolescence* (4th ed.). St. Louis, MI: Elsevier. © 2012 by Mosby, an imprint of Elsevier; Sax, N. & Weston, E. (2007). *Language development milestones.* Available at http://www.rehabmed.ualberta.ca/spa/phonology/milestones.pdf

of age, infants' babbling includes the sounds of the primary language(s) of their environment. Some articulation errors are normative in early childhood; by middle childhood, typically developing children have no detectable difficulties with expressive phonology.

Children typically begin to demonstrate *phonological awareness* between age 2 and 3, when they become aware of rhyming. Around school age, phonological awareness increases as they start to be able to segment words into syllables and speech sounds, and to apply their phonological knowledge to reading and spelling; more sophisticated knowledge develops through to mid to late adolescence (Paul & Norbury, 2012).

Development of Semantics and Grammar

Infants are also primed to learn grammar and semantics, with exposure to sufficient consistent and complex language stimulation. Infants typically begin to understand single words during the first year and to speak their first word around age 1. Semantic development accelerates during the second year to approximately 200–300 words for typically developing children at 24 months (Ganger & Brent, 2004). Young children's ability to rapidly link new words with their meanings has been termed *fast mapping*. As this skill improves, supported by phonological and cognitive development, young children are able to learn words more readily, and their vocabulary growth increases (Gershkoff-Stowe & Hahn, 2007).

Children typically begin to combine words into two-word phrases around age 2. Young children acquire structural rules of their language and many word meanings without formal instruction. Acquisition of grammatical rules is acquired through rich exposure to language; adults support grammar learning by recasting (repeating corrected versions) of children's utterances. A sufficiently large vocabulary is needed to allow young children to absorb rules of grammar based on patterns in the languages they are exposed to in their environments.

Semantics and grammar develop together

Although grammar and semantics are separate domains, they develop in concert. Recent evidence demonstrates that young children use their semantic knowledge to understand grammar (semantic bootstrapping) and their knowledge of grammar to make inferences about word meanings (syntactic bootstrapping). Thus, problems in one domain can affect the other. Genetic influences also appear to affect grammar and semantics jointly (Dionne, Dale, Boivin, & Plomin, 2003).

Grammar development continues through the school age years with increasingly complex syntax, particularly in academic contexts. Most grammatical forms are in place by middle childhood. Complexity and variety of expressive syntax increase through late childhood and adolescence, and a few tenses increase in usage; the full range of adult syntax is generally in place by age 18 (Paul & Norbury, 2012). In contrast, semantic development progresses through adolescence and can continue through the life span as new words and concepts are learned, although the pace of development tends to slow after adolescence (Beitchman et al., 2008).

Pragmatic Development

Pragmatic skills develop through experience of social interaction. Caregivers' nonverbal and verbal communication introduce social and instrumental functions of language through repeated interactions in different contexts. Infants learn pragmatic skills such as *turn taking* through play and other interactions with caregivers. Later in their first year, infants begin to use *gestures* and *vocalizations* to intentionally communicate.

Pragmatic development continues as children's linguistic repertoire increases. Children develop pragmatic skills in context, as they experience the consequences of various communication strategies; as well as from direct instruction from caregivers. Pragmatic development overlaps with social development; learning how to use language effectively is a central part of learning how to interact with others. In addition, some aspects of pragmatics rely on cognitive development. For example, the ability to take into account knowledge of the listener and give appropriate context requires theory of mind understanding and perspective-taking abilities. More complex pragmatic skills (e.g., persuasion and exposition) are addressed in educational settings. Pragmatic development can continue into adulthood, as adults may seek to improve their communication skills for particular purposes.

2.1.2   Environmental Support for Language Learning

Language is generally acquired without formal instruction, as long as the child is exposed to rich, fully complex language with sufficient language stimulation. However, this statement glosses over the countless social interactions that typically support language development. Infants' participation in these interactions become increasingly active and intentional; however, the active participation of caregivers continues to be pivotal in supporting language development. For example, the experience of *joint attention* – the infant and caregiver attending to the same thing, is an important facilitator for language learning as it allows objects or events to be discussed.

Parents and caregivers often engage with young children in a manner that supports language development. For example, *conversational recasts* (repeating back a corrected version of the child's utterance), and *expansions* (repeating back an expanded version of the child's utterance), which many parents do routinely in their interactions with young children, is a technique used in speech therapy to support development.

The quality and quantity of parents' interactions with children accounts for considerable variance in children's language development (Glascoe & Leew, 2010; Hoff, 2006). Cohen (2001) noted that the same parenting skills that foster secure attachment also foster language development: responsiveness and following the child's lead. Research supports this, showing that child-directed speech that elicits conversation is associated with more rapid language development in comparison with speech to control the child's behavior. In addition, factors such as *quantity of speech* directed to young children, *variety of words used,* and *grammatical complexity* are associated with rates of language acquisition. Book reading is especially important to language growth because it elicits language from caregivers that is especially conducive to language development: complex language, pedagogical strategies, and discussion of words and language. Differences in parental language use by socioeconomic status (SES) disappear in the book reading context (Hoff, 2006).

Peer interaction is also a necessary (though not sufficient) context for language development as it provides opportunities for language uses including storytelling, negotiation, and conflict resolution to a greater extent than other contexts (Hoff, 2006).

2.1.3   Critical / Sensitive Periods

It is well known that learning a new language becomes much more difficult with age, particularly after early adolescence. Less well known is the importance of constant and consistent exposure to rich language stimulation *in any language* during the first few years of life for language development. Which language an infant / young child is exposed to is much less important than opportunities to communicate with an expert speaker who uses the full range of linguistic complexity of the language. Language and related cognitive abilities, such as fast mapping (the ability to quickly link words and meanings) may not develop as well in children who did not experience early, consistent rich language stimulation (Glascoe & Leew, 2010).

Knowledge Needs of Parents
Parents and caregivers may not be fully aware of the importance of consistent exposure to rich language, especially in early infancy, nor of caregivers' roles in promoting infant language acquisition. This is not surprising given that language learning occurs without formal instruction and may therefore appear "automatic." Research suggests that many parents assume their levels of interaction are sufficient for optimal language development. However, these parents were open to learning about fostering language development when informed of the extent to which infants are primed to learn language from birth and benefit from high levels of interaction especially in the critical periods of infancy and early childhood (National Literacy Trust, 2010). This information may be particularly important for parents of children with language difficulties, and may benefit younger siblings at increased risk of speech, language, or reading difficulties due to shared genetic and/or environmental risk.

2.2   Language Impairment / Language Disorders

The causes of LI are not well known. In fact, cases with clear etiological factors are excluded from most definitions of LI. Nevertheless, potential causal or contributing factors for LI have been identified. Both the heterogeneity of individuals with LI, and the complexity and number of skills involved in verbal communication, support the idea that LI likely comprises multiple deficits arising from a combination of vulnerabilities. We discuss some etiological factors below.

Genetic Factors in Language Impairment (LI)

- Genetics of language impairment are complex, based on
  - Heterogeneity of LI phenotype
  - Range in heritability estimates for LI across studies
  - Different heritability for specific skills, e.g., nonword repetition
  - Nonspecific family history in broad speech/language/reading domain
  - Separate chromosomal linkages

- Heritability is greatest for
  - Phonological (speech) impairment
  - Children referred for speech/language services
  - Nonword repetition
  - Expressive language more than receptive language

- Gene/environment interactions may play a role

2.2.1   Genetics and Language Impairment

Genetic Factors

As discussed in Chapter 1, there is little agreement on appropriate definitions and cutoffs for language disorders. Nevertheless, studies have been conducted to attempt to assess the heritability of LI. Twin studies of children with specific language impairment have shown greater concordance for monozygotic twins than for dizygotic twins (Bishop, North, & Donlan, 1995; Lewis & Thompson, 1992; Tomblin & Buckwalter, 1994). However, heritability estimates have varied considerably across studies depending on how LI is defined (Bishop & Hayiou-Thomas, 2008). Heritability is higher when there is comorbid *phonological impairment*; phonological disorders are highly heritable, independent of LI. Heritability also appears higher for children clinically referred for speech/language services than for children identified based on standardized language measures. This finding could reflect comorbid phonological impairments, which are associated with clinical referrals; alternatively, it may rule out children whose LI is subthreshold (Bishop & Hayiou-Thomas, 2008). It is also possible that parents aware of a family history of language-related difficulties may be more likely to notice speech/language issues in their children and refer them for clinical services.

In non-twin studies, language difficulties appear to "run in families"; however, the genetic associations tend to be broad. For example, LI is associated with a family history of speech, language, or reading difficulties, rather than a family history of LI (Bishop, 1997).

Expressive language impairment appears more heritable than receptive language impairment. Nonword repetition is strongly heritable. DNA studies have identified distinct chromosomal linkages with skills related to LI (such as nonword repetition); these linkages are not strongly intercorrelated. Taken together, and given the heterogeneity of the LI phenotype, these findings suggest a complex genetic etiology, with multiple genetic as well as environmental factors, and potentially gene/environment interactions (Bishop & Hayiou-Thomas, 2008).

Neurological Factors

One pathway from genetic risk to LI is through neurological factors. A number of studies have investigated neurological correlates of LI, including brain structure and function. This research area is fairly new, and few clear results have emerged. In addition, broader issues of causality apply: Brain and/or processing differences between individuals with LI and typically developing peers may reflect neuroplasticity, developing in response to language difficulties, rather than causing them (Bishop, 2006).

2.2.2   Information Processing and Working Memory Limitations

Limitations in cognitive processing have been proposed as contributors to LI. First, *working memory systems* including *phonological short-term memory,* are essential for young children to acquire speech sounds, and the meanings of words and phrases (van Daal, Verhoeven, van Leeuwe, & van Balkom, 2008). LI is associated with working memory limitations. Children with LI appear to have capacity limitations in the amount of information that can be stored in the short term to be processed, and processing limitations in the complexity of task demands that can be met (Leonard et al., 2007).

A test of phonological short-term memory, nonword repetition, appears to be a reliable marker of LI (Bishop, 2006). The task involves memorizing nonword syllables (e.g., *blonterstaping*). Children with LI have more difficulty with longer stimuli, consistent with limitations in working memory capacity. This is important because language learning involves associating novel speech sounds with their meanings; phonological memory limitations can interfere with this process. Children with LI also may have particular difficulty generating verbal cues to help with processing tasks. For example, they have difficulty memorizing a set of picture cards because of problems generating labels that would allow them to organize and rehearse the information (Gillam & Hoffman, 2004).

Processing Speed

Processing speed is also related to language, as rapid processing of information is required for spoken language. On average, children with LI show slower information processing, even in comparison with younger typically developing children who have been matched by language functioning (Leonard et al., 2007). Children with LI are able to process more information if it is presented at a slower rate. This is important for clinical work and is useful information for caregivers.

Auditory Discrimination and Processing

Speech perception requires rapid processing of extremely complex auditory information, such as discrimination between different sounds, and classification of sounds (disregarding distinctions between sounds that are not meaningful in the language environment). Some children with specific LI have general difficulty with auditory processing not involving language, for instance, judging the order of high- and low-frequency tones presented at high speed. Auditory processing may be a factor for some children with LI; however, results have been inconsistent, and the direction of causality has not been established. For example, poor auditory processing may be a consequence rather than a cause of LI (Bishop, Hardiman, & Barry, 2012).

2.2.3   Hearing Impairment and Otitis Media

Because of the importance of consistent exposure to complex language, undetected hearing impairment can be a factor in language delay and/or impairment. Audiometry testing is important if any hearing impairment is suspected. Routine audiometry screens can identify hearing problems early so as not to interfere with language development. Transient hearing impairment, caused by ear infections (otitis media) was long thought to be related to LI. However, this appears to have been an artifact of referral bias (Bishop, 1997). There is no evidence that temporary hearing loss affects language development. Although persistent otitis media may be a risk factor for language impairment, particularly in combination with other factors, this has not been clearly established (Rovers, Schilder, Zielhuis, & Rosenfeld, 2004).

2.2.4   Environmental Factors

It is widely acknowledged that various environmental factors play a role in the development of LI. *Socioeconomic status* (SES) and a variety of indicators related to social disadvantage and family challenges and distress are associated with LI. Given the importance of high levels of language stimulation for language acquisition and development, it is not surprising that indicators of decreased parental/family resources, increased family stressors, and poorer parenting skills would be associated with child language difficulties.

In interpreting the association between social disadvantage and LI, there is a potential for confounding environmental effects with genetic associations. In biological families, parents with poorer language skills may have lower SES and lower educational attainment as a result of their language disabilities.

However, support for the importance of environmental impacts on language learning has come from research showing that caregiver communication to infants and young children is associated with socioeconomic variables, most notably maternal education. Children with lower SES background are exposed to considerably less language input than are more privileged children. Quantity as well as quality of language input is associated with language development (Hart & Risley, 1995; Hoff, 2006). Other research has found that maternal education and sensitivity, both of which are correlated with SES, predict language outcomes. Maternal *child-directed speech* can account for the relation between SES and language outcomes.

Research also suggests that the association between psychosocial stressors and child language outcomes may also be accounted for to some extent by their impact on caregiver communication. Maternal depression is associated with lower levels of language input and outcomes, and may partly account for associations between language and psychopathology (Hoff, 2006; Le Paro, Justice, Skibbe, & Pianta, 2004).

Although linked to environmental factors, language development is robust – most children become expert speakers. This includes children in cultures with very different parenting practices. Language outcomes are due to a combination of factors related to language mechanisms and environmental factors; how these factors interact is not yet known.

2.3   Models Linking LI and Psychosocial Outcomes

Because of the importance of language in all aspects of life, LI may have an impact in multiple life domains across development. The following are some of the pathways by which LI may contribute to psychosocial and mental health concerns, arranged by their approximate developmental timing.

2.3.1   Parent–Child Relationships

Sensitive parenting fosters both psychosocial and language development

Language is key to social interactions; this is particularly true with respect to interactions with parents and other caregivers. Language acquisition usually takes place in the context of parent–child relationships; the qualities of parenting (e.g., sensitivity and ability to follow the child's lead) that support optimal language development in infancy and early childhood are the same qualities associated with other positive psychosocial outcomes including *secure attachment, adjustment,* and *competence* (Cohen, 2001). Thus, a common factor that may account for some of the association between LI and psychosocial outcomes may be parenting: both parenting skills and sufficient resources to be able to put these skills into practice. This is especially important for children with neurocognitive vulnerabilities.

Adults often overestimate children's comprehension. Apparently uncooperative or oppositional behavior may result from not understanding instructions or contexts

The child's language abilities can have an impact on the parent–child relationship. As they are learning language, young children can experience some frustration when they are unable to make themselves understood. Language difficulties can make this situation more frequent, and the language learning process may be more challenging and less rewarding for parents, who may in turn respond less positively to their children (Cohen, 2001). This does not mean that parents should be in any way blamed for their children's language impairments; children may have significant genetic and/or neurocognitive vulnerabilities, and their parents may have mitigated their impacts. However, parenting is amenable to intervention, and is therefore an area to consider in working with families.

2.3.2   Unrecognized Comprehension Problems

Adults often overestimate children's comprehension, even with typically developing children. This is much more problematic with children with language difficulties, who may understand considerably less of what is being said than adults realize. Further, their lack of comprehension of speech leads to more general difficulties in interpreting novel situations and contexts. Children may be assumed to be uncooperative, disobedient, or oppositional when they have not understood specific instructions or the broader context.

There are a number of negative consequences if parents, teachers, and others adults in the child or youth's life do not understand the source of their difficulties. First, the child's problems or needs in a given situation are not able to be addressed (e.g., when the child does not understand the task demands in a school assignment); second, the child experiences behavioral failure in the classroom or home situation, which may compound coexisting academic difficulties. Third, negative expectations about the child can carry over into other situations, especially as such misunderstandings are likely to reoccur.

In addition to affecting the child's self-concept, consistent experiences of failure in the school environment can make it more difficult to a child to remain engaged with school, which can lead to disruptive behavior. The child's experience of being consistently misread may also interfere with the *parent–child attachment relationship*. Further, with consistent misattributions of noncompliance, escalating *coercive patterns* may develop between caregiver and child, which can also be associated with disruptive behavior problems (Patterson, DeBaryshe, & Ramsey, 1989). Alternatively, children may withdraw or express anxiety and distress when they do not understand the context. Withdrawal in particular can be interpreted as shyness, and language difficulties may be missed. This is especially likely among girls with LI.

Consistent experiences of failure can interfere with school engagement compounding academic difficulties

Ongoing consequences of a child's language difficulties may undermine the parent–child relationship

2.3.3   Self-Regulation

Language is intimately tied to emotional development and self-regulation. From an early age, young children learn to use language to communicate their concerns. In preschool and early school years, learning to express feelings and desires rather than acting out is a common educational goal. Communication competence reduces frustration and supports the ability to tolerate delayed gratification as young children learn to communicate their desires before they are met. This in turn supports other aspects of emotional regulation.

Young children also use self-talk as a form of self-regulation, at first talking to themselves aloud, then internally. Young children under 10 direct a large proportion of utterances to themselves, especially in problem-solving situations (Berk, 1992). Self-talk is used to guide their actions; children talk themselves through more challenging parts of activities they are working on, sometimes repeating suggestions of adult mentors. Self-talk is especially likely when children are working at the edge of their current skill level – or *zone of proximal development* (Diaz & Berk, 1992; Vygotsky, 1962).

Children with learning disabilities, attention problems, and environments with relatively low levels of parental conversation lag behind their peers in their use of self-talk (Berk, 1992). Children with language impairment may have more difficulty using self-talk to support their problem solving due to linguistic challenges (Sturn & Johnston, 1999).

Private speech is linked to self-regulation more broadly; using private speech, children learn to control their own behavior. Verbal self-regulation is associated with the development of *executive function* skills. Youths with language impairment may have deficits in executive function due to difficulties with verbal mediation and self-regulation.

2.3.4   Social Problems

Language is an important aspect of peer interaction starting in early childhood. Children with LI may have more difficulty navigating social situations due to comprehension difficulties in social interactions, and more general misunderstanding of situations and contexts. Children with pragmatic difficulties have particular difficulties with social interactions. Those who have not been identified with severe pragmatic difficulties but have LI may nevertheless find it more difficult than others to enter conversations or respond in novel situations due to their difficulties with comprehension and expression (Fujiki et al., 1999).

Children and adolescents with language impairment are more likely to be rejected by their peers

In addition, peers are sensitive to language functioning. Children with expressive language difficulties may have poorer communication skills and are more likely to be rejected by their peers. This may be partly due to concomitant social skills difficulties. For older children and youths, language is an increasingly important part of peer socialization. Youths with language difficulties may not be able to participate fully in banter or verbal exchanges; this also reduces opportunities for peer interactions, which play a unique role in language development (Hoff, 2006). This can be a long-standing problem, as the language skills of children with LI continue to lag behind those of others. (Durkin & Conti-Ramsden, 2010).

Adults also respond more negatively to children with poorer language skills (even when the domain of language is not highlighted, and they are not aware of the children's language disorders). This can compound the social difficulties LI children face, as they may be less likely to be supported by an adult (e.g., Rice et al., 1993).

2.3.5   Academic Achievement Issues and Competence

Language impairment can increase the challenge of any academic subject

LI is associated with academic difficulties in a number of domains. These difficulties show up both in lower school grades and poorer scores on standardized academic achievement tests. Academic performance in reading and language is most impaired by a language disorder; however, virtually all academic subjects have a linguistic component and use verbal instruction and reading materials. Poorer performance in math and other domains is common in children with LI (Young et al., 2002). Children with LI have been shown to have more difficulties acquiring new words; this presents an ongoing challenge as new vocabulary is introduced in different subject areas (Alt & Plante, 2006; Rice, Oetting, Marquis, Bode, & Pae, 1994; Williams; 2010). Reading difficulties are very common among individuals with LI (Catts, Fey, Zhang, & Tomblin, 1999; Snowling, Bishop, & Stothard, 2000; Young et al., 2002). Again, not all would meet criteria for a learning disability; however, poorer reading skills present academic challenges. If the LI is unidentified, this decreases the likelihood that the delivery of the curriculum will be adapted to address language difficulties.

Persistent difficulties with school performance may lead to decreased confidence and self-esteem. In addition, children with LI may experience chronic stress related to school, particularly as linguistic demands increase – that is, in secondary school. Public speaking (presentations, etc.) may be a particular source of anxiety. In late adolescence, LI is associated with social phobia, particularly related to situations involving speaking (Voci et al., 2006).

Academic performance is associated with skill development over and above academic subjects. Children who are having difficulties may be less engaged and may not have the same opportunity to benefit from educational experiences, and related organizational, social, communication, community membership, teamwork, and other skills, as children who are academically strong. Communication difficulties provide an additional barrier to full school participation. Academic performance is also associated with later career opportunities; these may be restricted to the extent that academic problems are not remedied.

Academic performance may be especially important among children with additional psychosocial risk factors or stressors, which are somewhat more common among youths with LI. Academic achievement has been shown to be associated with adaptation and resilience among vulnerable youths. For youths with mental health concerns or vulnerability due to psychosocial stressors and environmental disadvantages, strong academics are a protective factor, associated with positive outcomes (Masten et al., 2004).

There is a large literature linking language/verbal deficits to externalizing problems and, in particular, delinquency. Academics may partially mediate the relation between language impairment and delinquency. Two theories have been proposed to account for the association between school achievement problems and antisocial outcomes. First, *disengagement from school* leads the youth away from prosocial contexts, goals, and peers. Second, education does not provide rewards for the youth who experiences failure and conflict; involvement in delinquent activity may offer alternative sources of reward, including economic rewards, if career success does not appear attainable (Brownlie et al., 2004)

Ongoing school performance difficulties can undermine confidence and self-esteem

3

Diagnosis and Treatment Indications

3.1   Diagnostic Approach

For ease of presentation, the assessment of speech and language development and the assessment of emotional and behavioral concerns are presented separately. In practice, the order will partly depend on the nature of the presenting complaints and these are often integrated in the course of the enquiry with the parents and the child. Begin with an assessment of speech and language development when these are the leading concerns, otherwise start with the behavioral and emotional issues.

As many as 50% of children presenting at mental health clinics with behavioral and emotional problems have language delays (Cohen et al., 1993, 1998). These language delays may have a direct bearing on the nature of the child's behavior problems and, importantly, may be a key factor in successful treatment.

Any family experiencing distress associated with their child's language, learning, emotions, or behavior should have their child assessed

The most common clinical presentations are language impairment (LI) with comorbid DBDs, including ADHD, oppositional defiant disorder (ODD), and conduct disorder (CD), and LI and comorbid anxiety disorders. There are many cases with subclinical symptomatology that do not fulfill the criteria for a psychiatric diagnosis; the child and or family are nevertheless experiencing levels of distress that warrant intervention. The younger child, especially a preschooler, is more likely to present because of delayed language development. Behavioral and emotional concerns may be present or emerging, but the parental focus is usually the delayed language development. See Appendices 1–4 for report forms for anxiety (parent report), ADHD, CD, and ODD symptoms (parent/teacher report).

It is essential to determine whether the child's language development is proceeding normally or whether there is evidence of delayed language development. Given the complexity and the subtlety of language development and delays, problems with phonological processing, language comprehension, auditory memory, and auditory discrimination tend to be invisible and are more easily overlooked. These impairments may also coexist with delayed expression or problems with articulation which are more visible and will bring the child to the attention of the parents, teachers, or other adults. Because phonological processing is highly correlated with reading, you will need to be alert to these issues, advising the parents to monitor the child's progress in reading if the child's phonological skills are delayed.

The initial interviews are used to gather information on the nature of the child's symptoms and the presenting concerns or complaint. Detailed information on the history of the symptoms or problems, the circumstances in which they occur, and the child's developmental progress socially and academically are noted. Audiometric testing to check for hearing impairment should be considered for any child suspected of suboptimal hearing or who has a history of repeated otitis media. Information about the child's areas of strength, competence, and interests is obtained, as are the nature of the family and social supports available to the child. Discussion with the parents regarding their personal and family history of language development and any mental health concerns must be part of the enquiry.

An initial task is to establish the nature and extent of the child's language delays if any, with particular reference to phonological processing and receptive and expressive language including grammar, semantics, and pragmatics. The clinician must also be attentive to and diagnose any emotional or behavioral problems that are part of the clinical presentation. Until proven otherwise it is best to assume an association between language impairment and any comorbid conditions or problems. An important diagnostic and therapeutic challenge is to discover and clarify the nature of the association, if any, between the child's language delays and these comorbidities when present.

Initial task is to describe areas of difficulty or deficit: namely, language functioning and any behavioral or emotional symptoms

The assessment of the child's language development begins with a careful developmental history. Ask the parents when the child spoke in single words, when the child was able to put two or three words together to express himself/herself. A parent reported checklist can be a useful tool for collecting this information; parental concern can also identify language delay or impairment (see Section 1.7). Any evidence of delay or a family history of learning disabilities / delayed language development raises the risk that the child may be language impaired and should be referred to a speech-language pathologist for a speech and language assessment. A screening tool, such as a sentence repetition task (see Section 1.7), can also quickly identify language difficulties that require assessment and may otherwise be missed.

The assessment of the child's language development must also attend to the child's pragmatic competencies such as turn taking, conversational repair, eye contact, understanding the perspective of others, as well as conversational tone and prosody, for example. However, pragmatic impairments are not restricted to spoken language and encompass social, emotional, and communicative aspects of social interaction (Adams, Baxendale, Lloyd, & Aldred, 2005) that are considered inappropriate for the social context – for instance laughing when told of someone's death, blurting out embarrassing comments without due recognition of their impact on the other person, and being out of step with others' meaning and intent in social interactions. These are examples that suggest pragmatics impairment, however, there continues to be disagreement about which children have primary pragmatic impairments (Botting & Conti-Ramsden 1999).

Pragmatic difficulties occur in a variety of clinical psychiatric syndromes, such as ADHD (Leonard, Milich, & Lorch, 2011) and most notably in autism spectrum disorders. Rapin and Allen (1987) used the term semantic-pragmatic disorder to refer to children with autism, although this usage is not currently endorsed. There is abundant evidence, however, that not all children with pragmatic difficulties have autism (Botting & Conti-Ramsden, 1999). Some have argued that there is no sharp dividing line between children with pragmatic language impairments and autism (Bishop & Norbury, 2002). The addition of the DSM-5 diagnosis social (pragmatic) communication disorder introduces a diagnostic category for children with pragmatic language impairments who do not meet the full criteria for an autism spectrum disorder (American Psychiatric Association, 2013). Because pragmatic difficulties are a diagnostic feature of autism spectrum disorder, the differential diagnosis between an autism spectrum disorder and a language disorder, including social (pragmatic) communication disorder, is based on the presence, severity, and pervasiveness of stereotyped behavior symptoms such as restricted, repetitive stereotyped behaviors, interests, and activities found in the autism spectrum but not with language disorders. These restricted, repetitive patterns of behavior are usually manifest in the early development period; therefore a complete history should be obtained before considering the diagnosis of social (pragmatic) communication disorder.

Unless proven otherwise it is best to assume some level of pragmatic difficulty among children with delayed language development. Careful discussion with the parents and teachers will usually identify situations in which the pragmatic difficulties arise. The clinical interview can be helpful as well in noting the degree to which the child is responsive and appropriately interactive. The clinical interview should not be used to rule out pragmatic difficulties without collateral information because some children can relate to an adult in the context of an interview but nevertheless struggle to relate to their peers.

3.2   Treatment Indications

LI children present in several different ways:

(1) **Initial presentation with identified language problem**
   (a) The child's acquisition of expressive language is delayed and treatment is sought.
   (b) The child appears to have difficulty responding to oral instructions.

(2) **Initial presentation for behavioral and/or emotional disorder**
   (a) Child described as shy and socially inhibited, with difficulties making friends.
   (b) Child described as "spacy" easily distracted, and has difficulty attending to classroom academics.
   (c) Child is struggling with reading and tends to be impulsive.
   (d) Child has difficulty with transitions, becomes rigid, oppositional, and behaviorally challenging when required to change activities.
   (e) Child is noted to be socially awkward, with difficulty engaging in socially appropriate reciprocal social relationships.
   (f) Child noted to be reactive in social situations and quickly becomes upset.

3.2.1   Guidance

Initial Presentation With Identified Language Problem

Child's Acquisition of Expressive Language Is Delayed and Treatment Is Sought
For the child presenting with expressive language delays, the nature and extent of the child's language delays, with particular reference to phono-

logical processing and articulation, and receptive and expressive language, including, vocabulary, grammar, semantics, and pragmatics, must be clarified. It would be unusual for a child to show solitary delays in expressive language without delays in any other aspect of communication. The specific language profile should be reviewed and discussed with the parents and the child, and treatment should be targeted to the specific area of deficit. Once these parameters are known, treatment can be organized to target the identified areas of delay.

Three initial goals of treatment:
(1) Reduce the gap between the child's language level and that of typically developing children.
(2) Educate parents regarding possible later developing comorbid disorders.
(3) Advise parents to be proactive to minimize risks of comorbid disorders

Treatment may have several goals: First, it is intended to reduce the gap between the child's current level of language development and that of typically developing children; second, the parents are provided with an understanding of the implications of the child's language delays, and the need to be vigilant for the development of subsequent comorbid conditions, such as an anxiety disorder or upon school entry, evidence of attentional problems or a reading disability; third, the parents can be alerted and take steps to minimize the occurrence of comorbid conditions – by, for example, working with school personnel for special educational programming.

Any discussion of the risks, challenges, and outcomes must be placed in the context of the child's strengths, the family's strengths, and the presence of a supportive social network.

The therapist/clinician must negotiate the specific goals of treatment with the child and the child's parents. In this context, it is important to set realistic goals, and to target problems or symptoms identified by the child or family that are amenable to intervention. A related goal of treatment is to help the parents and the child understand that the language delay is not because the child is lazy or oppositional, nor is it due to their misbehavior. This alone can be therapeutic in helping to modify parental attitudes toward the child and lead to improved parent–child relationships.

Child Appears to Have Difficulty Responding to Oral Instructions

Johnny does not listen to me. He does not do what I ask him to. This is one of parents' most common complaints. You will need to determine whether this is due to delays in the child's language development, attributable to behavioral challenges in the parent–child relationship, or due to the child's behavior disorder. The answer to this question will guide the intervention strategy.

You must determine whether or not the child's language development is delayed. The child's hearing must be assessed, and if found to be problematic, referral to the appropriate specialist is in order. If the child's hearing is unimpaired, the child's expressive and receptive language should be evaluated. Once this information is known, the specific areas of deficit can be targeted and the family informed of the child's areas of competence and deficits.

Problems in responding to oral instructions may be because of the child's auditory memory limitations, such that the child is unable to retain more than one, simple instruction at a time. The child may have problems with auditory discrimination and have difficulty processing oral instruction when the spoken words are delivered more quickly than the child can process and retain. This is not intended to be an exhaustive list, but an example of the complex reasons for a child to have trouble responding to oral instructions.

Treatment with the child will target the specific areas of deficit. For example, the child's grammatical understanding may be delayed, this in turn interferes with his/her ability to understand time and causal sequences, and consequently the child is confused about the order in which events are to transpire. The child may need help remembering oral instructions involving more than one step. Practicing and rehearsing and repeating instructions softly to oneself can help improve performance. In addition to working directly with the child, treatment can focus on instructing parents to break down instructions into smaller bits, to ask the child to repeat what was said, thus to ensure the parent has the child's attention when given oral instructions.

Initial Presentation for Behavioral and/or Emotional Disorder

Child Is Described as Shy and Socially Inhibited, With Difficulties Making Friends

There may be many reasons the child has difficulty making friends – for instance, he or she may have few shared interests or be geographically separated, with limited transportation opportunities. However, children with expressive and or receptive language delays are at increased risk of interpersonal difficulties; they have difficulties making friends (Kamhi, Masterson, & Apel, 2007).

The child with delayed expressive language may be subject to teasing, may lack the linguistic skills to interact with peers in socially appropriate ways and consequently feel intimidated by peers and reluctant to engage with them verbally and socially, and will avoid joining play groups or remain on the periphery of peer activities.

Evaluate for a language or learning disorder in any child who is anxious about attending school

A variety of symptoms suggestive of anxiety about attending school appear in the form of stomachaches, dizziness, headaches, and complaints of feeling unwell in the morning prior to leaving for school, or these may reoccur repeatedly, followed by a quick recovery once the child knows he/she will not be attending school. These signal the need for assessment and intervention. The assessment should guide the approach to intervention, but in most circumstances, it will begin by targeting the anxiety symptoms.

With younger children and in circumstances in which the symptoms of anxiety are less prominent or acute, therapy can focus on developing discourse management skills, such as topic initiation, topic maintenance, turn taking, requesting, commenting, responding, and others. The goal is to equip the child with social skills to facilitate his/her engagement with peers.

In parallel with any speech and language therapy the child receives, school personnel should be briefed on the issues and assist in supporting the child during free time, and if possible after school. School personnel can do a great deal to assist children subject to teasing and bullying. Schools can provide supervised play groups in which children are taught to accept differences in others, to make kindness and cooperation a virtue and desirable goal. Greater emphasis on the school culture that promotes positive values and eschews the negative behavior would propel schools into a new and desirable forward-looking future. Those socially inhibited children who also have an anxiety disorder should also be offered CBT for their anxiety symptoms.

Child Is Described as "Spacy," Easily Distracted, and Has Difficulty Attending to Classroom Academics

The child identified as having attention deficit disorder (ADD) who appears to be distractible and has difficulty concentrating in class may have unrecognized language comprehension or auditory memory problems. The child should be tested to confirm or rule out these concerns. In the circumstances when these concerns are confirmed, the child should have an individual education plan in which adjustments are made given the child's difficulties with orally presented material. More time for orally presented material or greater use of written or visually presented material should be made available. Providing these children with a synopsis of the material to be taught, ahead of time, may help familiarize them with some of the content and concepts, thereby helping them to follow and attend to the oral presentation

The child identified with attention and concentration problems in class may have unrecognized language comprehension or auditory memory problems

Other strategies can be tailored to the specific language deficits the child shows. For example, the child's vocabulary development may be delayed and contribute to his/her challenges understanding the material presented in class. In this instance, treatment would target vocabulary development.

If this child is also diagnosed with ADD or ADHD, then the appropriate treatment targeting this specific Axis 1 condition should be provided. Depending on the specific issues of the individual case, intervention may consist of parent training and CBT, either alone or in combination with medication. These issues are discussed in greater detail in the next section.

Child is Struggling With Reading and Tends to be Impulsive

Parents bring their child for an assessment because the teacher complains that their child does not pay attention in class, he/she is restless, bothers other children, and is behind in reading.

This is a common profile, and there is a high probability of a diagnosis of ADHD in this case. The behavioral symptoms can be attributed to ADHD, as

---

Clinical Pearl
Addressing Unrealistic Expectations

Look for the mismatch between unrealistic parental expectations and abilities based on the child's age, cognitive abilities, and developmental level. This dynamic presents as parental anger and frustration and a child who may present as depressed, apathetic, anxious, or oppositional. The specific diagnostic picture depends on the child's temperament and the nature of the parent–child interaction. Careful assessment of the child's cognitive abilities and developmental level sets the stage for intervention focused on parental education. Individual intervention for the child may be indicated, but the decision to intervene is best determined based on the child's profile of symptoms and the response to the therapeutic intervention with the parents. When school-based academic problems are identified, assessment for learning disabilities may result in recommendations for an individual education plan.

can the reading difficulties. However, there is good evidence (Werry, Elkind, & Reeves, 1987) that these symptoms can also be attributed to delayed language development. Consequently the assessment must consider both the possibility of ADHD as well as delayed language development. Other possibilities, such as depression or anxiety, may also be considered, though they would be less likely as explanations for the behavior picture.

Discuss the benefits and risks of medication for any child with comorbid LI and ADHD

The child may need an individual education plan. Moving the child to a smaller class with a better teacher to student ratio, together with reading remediation may result in enough support for the child so that the behavior is no longer problematic. Alternatively, the assessment may reveal the need for medication to address the ADHD symptoms. Depending on the severity of the child's symptoms – for instance, the presence of concomitant oppositional defiant behavior – additional psychosocial intervention may be necessary.

Child Has Difficulty With Transitions, Becomes Rigid, Oppositional, and Behaviorally Challenging When Required to Change Activities

Some children with receptive language delays experience difficulties with transitions. Parents and teachers report that the child will become upset, may have tantrums, or otherwise become behaviorally challenging when required to transition to another situation or activity.

These children have difficulty generalizing from the specific item or event to the class of items or events. They are concrete in their thinking and have difficulty shifting psychological sets. In addition, because they are language delayed, and language is the code by which we represent our environment internally, their internal representations may not be coherent or readily accessed; consequently, they can experience any change as disorienting and upsetting as though the world that they knew and depended upon was now unrecognizable.

Therapy targets the child's environment as well as helping the child to learn to accept alternatives to the item of interest or the particular situation. Parents and teachers should be briefed on the nature of the child's difficulties and advised to prepare the child as much as possible for any anticipated changes in the child's daily routines at home and school. Where possible, the teacher or parent should demonstrate the anticipated changes and review them with the child. One 7-year-old girl would get extremely upset when the play activity ended. In the therapeutic encounter, instead of warning her that the session was to end in a few minutes, she was told that they were soon coming to the "to be continued time" – this seemed to be a sufficient bridge to the next appointment and helped reduce the feelings of loss that the session was ending.

Strategies of self-talk and rehearsal to help build internal representations of bridges between situations can be helpful. Other strategies include helping the child to verbalize his/her emotions: "this makes me feel … sad, mad, worried etc." These are intended to help the child convert behavioral outbursts into more age-appropriate verbal expressions and acquire the ability of emotional self-regulation.

Child Is Noted to be Socially Awkward, With Difficulty Engaging in Socially Appropriate Reciprocal Social Relationships

The child who is socially awkward will not ordinarily seek treatment, but the child's awkwardness will be of concern to the child's parents, teachers, and other adults who know the child. It is not always possible to discern the reasons for the child's social difficulties. Diagnostically it is important to establish the level of the child's language competence, with specific reference to his/her semantic pragmatic development. Case Vignette 1 illustrates some of these issues.

Case Vignette 1

Behavioral and Social Difficulties Due to Delayed Language Comprehension and Expression

O.'s parents complained that he did not listen. At school, his teachers said he was easily distracted, and disrupted the other children. O. was a tall, handsome boy, who looked a little older than his 6 years would suggest. He was friendly and tried to be cooperative. He often appeared to have a vacuous smile. He appeared preoccupied and inattentive, and would not answer questions but simply responded by repeating what he had said, and might scream loudly and jump up and down when excited. He was easily excited, and became silly and spoke out of context. O. had great difficulty playing with other children and would be teased by them, and would often respond by screaming and laughing, and encouraging the other children to do the same.

O. had marked problems with language comprehension and expression. When asked, "What is a camera?" he said, "Say cheese." He also had word retrieval problems and would struggle to find the word for rocket finally calling it "magic power." He would make associations with a word or phrase and continue to perseverate.

He often seemed tangential in his thought, and would show inappropriate responses to questions. For example, in the midst of a totally unrelated discussion, he might blurt out, "The toilet is cracked and white stuff is coming out." One of his favorite statements was, "what a lovely bouquet," which he would repeat, and usually without reference to anything that was happening at the time. This would make him seem bizarre, odd, or silly to the other children and puzzle the adults who were trying to understand him.

Here is an example in which obvious behavioral and social difficulties can be traced to delayed language comprehension and expression. Clarifying the extent of the child's language difficulties is the first step in organizing appropriate intervention. Treatment is directed at his language comprehension, and concomitantly ensuring that his environment is tailored to his particular needs. For example, he will need increased individual supervision in social situations, and he will do better in small groups, and with individual instruction.

In some instances, especially with older children, the child is more aware of his/her difficulties in social situations and becomes anxious simply anticipating social situations. Therapy directed at the social anxiety would be an appropriate intervention.

Some children with a similar cognitive profile will become emotionally reactive in social situations. This can occur if the child feels humiliated, believes he/she is being exploited, or made fun of, or otherwise feels he/she is being treated unfairly.

Child Is Noted to be Reactive in Social Situations and Quickly Becomes Upset

The challenge here is to understand the reasons for the child's reactivity in social situations. Careful attention to the specific situations in which the child overreacts is needed to clarify whether the child misunderstands the communicative intent in terms of the content of the communication as well as the implied affective message.

The child or youth in this situation may have trouble with auditory discrimination, auditory memory, and or language comprehension. The target of therapy would be to clarify the nature of the language deficit and inform the child, youth, and parents. This alerts the individual to his/her deficits so as to take corrective action by being primed to ask questions to ensure comprehension and by alerting the interlocutor of the requirements for successful oral communication with the youth.

Knowledge of the specific deficits allows more targeted interventions. This may mean a focus on vocabulary, or targeted practice with auditory discrimination, for example. Here too, to assist with behavioral control, self-talk, and the identification and verbal expression of emotions in the specific situation would be targets of treatment.

Delayed language development may be a factor in the child's difficulties in social situations. The child may have difficulty recognizing and expressing his/her own emotions verbally, and instead resorts to physical action instead. The child may also have difficulty recognizing the emotions of others and consequently misjudges the intent of others, or is otherwise socially inappropriate, leading to altercations. CBTs targeting these specific issues would be the recommended approach. Depending on the response to individual therapy and on the extent of the social difficulties, for some, individual therapies followed by group approaches would be the preferred treatment approach.

Cognitive behavioral approaches with the focus on identifying internal emotions and other's emotions and training in empathy are common therapeutic tactics. See the next section for further details.

Clinical Pearl
Identify Settings in Which Symptoms Occur

Identify the maintaining factors and separate them into those issues that arise within the family and home setting, those that are related to school-based performance, those in relation to peers and social situations, those that may be intrapersonal, and those that arise in multiple settings. The treatment goals are then articulated in relation to the setting in which they arise. For example, the child who is anxious about attending school because he/she is behind in reading and fears being embarrassed can be offered help with remedial reading and concurrently a brief course of CBT to help address the anxiety symptoms. Symptoms arising in multiple settings signal a more severe clinical picture and require more comprehensive intervention.

4

Treatment

4.1   Methods of Treatment

Language impairment can be diagnosed and described according to diagnostic criteria such as the DSM-5 and the ICD-10. LI can also be described dimensionally, reflecting the level of functioning attained or the severity of impairment. In addition, various components of language competence can be measured, such as phonological skills, language comprehension, auditory memory, expressive language, etc. Consequently a child's language competence can be assessed and reported in terms of its level, as well as with respect to specific components.

LI is associated with fundamental aspects of cognitive functioning so that with increasingly severe LI, more aspects of cognitive abilities, such as working memory, or attentional processes, increasingly become affected. This in turn has ripple effects on multiple aspects of the child's daily functioning, at home, at school, and with peers.

Except for the very young child prior to school entry or the child with mild language impairments, a child with a pure language disorder without any other comorbid conditions would be quite rare. Additionally, LI interferes with effective communication, and this in turn can lead to social and psychological problems (teasing, being isolated and rejected, etc). Also, LI is a strong risk factor for reading failure, which carries its own set of risk factors for psychiatric disorders, such as conduct disorder and antisocial behavior. Depending on the severity and type of LI certain cognitive processes will be affected, such as memory or processing speed, for example. These in turn may contribute to the child's poor self-esteem, or problems acquiring valued skills, which can generate a cascade of untoward consequences leading to a variety of comorbid disorders, such as depression, anxiety, and conduct disorders.

4.1.1   General Treatment Guidelines

Therapeutic intervention is organized along three broad principles which are fundamental and inform all aspects of the therapeutic work with children and adolescents: (1) Intervention directed at the child's language competencies, in which therapy is focused on specific components of language will result in gains and improvement in these specific components, such as in phonological processing, for example; however evidence for substantive gains in fundamentals of language are more limited. (2) Consequently, an important aspect of intervention for the LI child is to make his/her environment more

---

Therapeutic Intervention

Therapeutic intervention is organized along three broad principles:

(1) Intervention directed at the child's language competencies;

(2) Intervention to adjust the environment to accommodate the child's needs;

(3) Intervention focused on therapy with the child (or youth) to equip him/ her with the knowledge and skills to redress the behavioral and emotional symptoms.

---

accommodating so that symptoms that arise secondarily as a consequence of the problems in communication are minimized. This would likewise be an important therapeutic approach with the LI child with a comorbid disorder. (3) There are obvious limitations to the extent to which the child's environment can be made more accommodating; consequently, a third therapeutic tack focuses on the child's behavior and emotional symptoms. Here the goal is to equip the child with the knowledge and skills to redress symptoms of anxiety and reduce or eliminate behavioral symptoms. This is accomplished through a variety of therapeutic approaches, such as individual therapies using cognitive behavior principles and therapies, parent training approaches, and social skills training. Because the LI child with a comorbid disorder ordinarily has symptoms in multiple settings such as at school, at home, and in the community, intervention will be most effective when it is comprehensive, with interventions at multiple levels and in multiple settings. The methods used and how they are delivered is the subject of this chapter.

4.1.2 Focus on Language

Most LI children show deficits in cognitive domains in addition to language; a comprehensive assessment of these will inform treatment

LI children may show deficits in domains other than language. Deficiencies in speed of processing and working memory are two aspects of cognitive development that have been found to be associated with LI (Leonard et al., 2007). In addition, poor frequency discrimination has also been associated with children with auditory processing difficulties and delayed language development. In planning intervention, attention to these aspects of the child's cognitive development is needed to inform the specific approach to intervention. For example, simply allowing more time or slowing the rate of presentation for the child with deficiencies in speed of processing will be helpful and lead to improvement in the child's performance.

Here are some strategies to assist the child or youth with speed of processing limitations. (Gillam & Hoffman, 2004):

(1) **Support attention:** To fully attend, the child or youth may need a period of preparation. Allow time for relevant information to be activated in memory. Present information several times, or, with youths, stress the relevance and importance of material before presenting it. Support selective attention, emphasize key messages, and eliminate distractions.

(2) **Support comprehension:** This gives the client more time to process information and reduces perceptual difficulty, which mitigates limitations with working memory and phonological processing.

(3) **Support organization:** Child or youth may need assistance in organizing information. Making lists or summaries helps them to internalize messages from the therapeutic work.

(4) **Support retention**: Provide handouts, or use props or other cues to assist with recall.

Some investigators have identified an auditory acoustic approach in which auditory components of speech and nonspeech stimuli such as rate, interstimulus interval, frequency, intensity, and presence of background noise, and other acoustic variables are manipulated in order to train the child's auditory perception, without regard to the content, meaning, or grammatical structures of the language. The contrasting approach focuses on spoken language, notably the content, meaning, and form. Evidence for the efficacy of the former approach is lacking; the latter is the more commonly used approach (Fey et al., 2011).

Recognizing the nature and extent of the child's language delays is a critical element in the ongoing therapy with the child. The results of the speech and language assessment or the psychological testing should provide a profile of the child's strengths and areas of deficit and how delayed or impaired the child is in that particular skill or ability.

Be sure to inform the parents and the child that you are recommending a comprehensive approach to intervention, and because the language difficulties are strongly associated with the child's behavioral and or emotional difficulties, the therapy must address both the speech and language problems and behavioral and emotional problems. Whether to offer therapy for the language difficulties and the behavioral and emotional problems in parallel or sequentially will depend on the reasons for referral and specific concerns identified. It will also depend on the severity of the child's communicative problems and whether without additional speech and language therapy he/she will be able to participate in the therapy for the behavioral or emotional problems. In organizing the treatment, caution should be exercised to avoid overprogramming or overscheduling the treatment sessions.

Younger children with delayed language development may not show evidence of psychiatric symptoms that are clinically significant, but they are at high risk of developing learning disabilities, anxiety disorders, and upon school entry, with increased demands to attend and concentrate in the classroom setting, symptoms consistent with ADD or ADHD may become more evident. Here the therapeutic targets should begin with the child's language delays. If the child is not yet in school, be sure to advise the parents to maintain a close liaison with the child's teacher so that signs of anxiety about school or peers can be dealt with early. Help with reading can be introduced at the first signs of trouble. Early intensive intervention for reading delays has been shown to be effective (Lovett, Barron, & Benson, 2003).

Once the child's language competencies are described treatment aimed at the specific language difficulties can be started. Speech/language therapy may involve individual sessions but alternate and supplementary approaches will include language facilitation techniques conducted by the parents with the support of the speech and language pathologist. This approach is most successful when the parents and the therapist are able to work together as a collaborative team, with guided practice and specific feedback provided by the speech language pathologist. Though not intended to be in a teacher–student relationship,

Table 10
Facilitating Child's Expressive Language: Levels of Support

Communication support	Examples	Comments
Closed and simple factual or preference questions	Do you want to play with the boat or the truck? Do you like to dance? What grade are you in? What's your favorite color? Do you have any pets? Did you feel happy or sad?	– Support communication by providing the expressive content – Requires primarily receptive language skills – Elicits less information than open questions – Clinician-led – Single concepts reduce processing demands – Assumptions in questions can risk alienating some youth
Verbal scaffolding of child or youth's narratives	What happened first? First they.... Then what happened? Then you... Then they...	– Clinician supports and encourages client's narratives by initiating the start of their responses – Supports child or youth's narrative production, attention, and persistence with the narrative – Can be used in client's recounting of experiences or in play or stories
Open-ended questions	What would you like to do? What happened? How did you feel? What do you like about [favorite activity]?	– Provides an intermediate level of support – Clinician sets the course of the discourse, but the child or youth responds more freely – Working at this level facilitates psychotherapeutic work, and supports increased comfort with expressive language
Facilitating expression	*Elicit response* Can you guess what's in here? Look what I found! *Give time* [Wait. If no response, stay on topic so youth has extended opportunity to respond]	– Attention-getting strategies appropriate for younger children – Elicits expression with less prompting – For older children/youth, give extended time to respond before moving on – Remaining on topic allows youth more time to respond without extended silence – Simplifies conversational skills required to enter into dialogue

Based on information from D. L. Williams (2010). *Developmental language disorders: Learning language and the brain.*

the therapist will need to offer some guidance and initial supervision while observing the parent interacting with their child. Modeling interventions and offering praise and encouragement when appropriate tend to be most favorably received. The therapist may act as a coach or consultant to the parents as they implement the therapy with their child; the speech and language therapist may also act as a cotherapist along with the parents.

Help the parents set realistic goals in the work with their child; there are no magic bullets, and the child with receptive language delays or problems with auditory memory will continue to have these challenges even though they progress and make gains. Greater progress will be evident with children who have expressive language difficulties with respect to articulation and phonological processing skills. Gains here will translate into gains in learning to read (Beitchman & Young, 1997; Lovett et al., 2003).

One of the key challenges in working therapeutically with individuals with language difficulties is to facilitate their verbal communication. This is pivotal for assessment and for working therapeutically with children. As already noted, difficulties in cognitive processing and working memory, and problems with language comprehension add to the demands of any verbal interchange and may be compounded when addressing emotionally loaded topics.

Engaging the LI child will require particular attention to the child's communicative competence and the need to use certain extra measures. Clinicians can use a number of methods to decrease the cognitive and linguistic demands for the child's verbal expression (Williams, 2010). Table 10 gives examples of a hierarchy of cues that can be used to support verbal communication. Being aware of the cognitive and communicative demands throughout the therapy session, the clinician can balance the amount of support needed, providing more support for some part of the session to build rapport and lessen the overall strain, while working to increase children's abilities to express themselves. Over time, higher levels of support may be less necessary.

Here is a conversational sample that illustrates some of the therapeutic techniques in working with a child with receptive and expressive LI.

Conversational sample between therapist (T.) and six-and-half-year-old Max:

Max: *Power ranger.*
T.: *What does it do?*
Max: *Walk.*
T.: *Wow.*
Max: *He's fight. He fight with tail.*
T.: *Oh my! Who does he fight?*
Max: *(gestures) Tail.*
T.: *He uses his tail. Who does he fight with?*
Max: *(gestures fighting)*
T.: *What show is he from?*
Max: *Movie power ranger. I have it.*
T.: *You're so lucky! Tell me about the movie.*
Max: *Yeah.*
T.: *What happened in the movie?*
Max: *Power ranger.*
T.: *What happened first?*

Max: *He's fight. He's fight. With tail.*

T.:   *Tell me more.*

Max: *He ... (points to teeth)*

T.:   *His teeth. Oh, scary.*

Max: *(no response)*

T.:   *He bites people. (gesturing biting) Ouch, biting hurts.*

Max: *Yeah.*

T.:   *Great toy, Max.*

In this example, the therapist provides scaffolding for the child – "what happened first." The therapist uses strategic pauses and encourages and invites the child to continue describing what he saw. The therapist also extends the child's utterance and elaborates it, giving the child the language to express his ideas.

4.1.3   Comorbid Language Disorders: Clarifying the Issues

We focus here on the treatment for the child with comorbid language and psychiatric disorders. The first principle in planning treatment is to correctly diagnose the nature of the problem.

The First Interview

The first interview focuses on obtaining a clear description of the concerns that led to the referral.

Meeting separately with the parents allows them to express fears and frustrations that would be inappropriate with the child present

Introduce yourself, describe the process of assessment, and advise the parent(s) that they will be seen separately and consequently to use their judgment on what to discuss with the child present when describing the reason for the referral and assessment. This is important because sometimes parents feel so exasperated with their child that they unleash a torrent of accusations, blame, and other demeaning comments. The child may have heard this before, but here we are trying to be therapeutic, and the message is that we do not blame or accuse, but seek to understand and offer guidance and treatment. In part this is the initial therapeutic foray – modeling a nonjudgmental attitude.

The child and parents are seen together, and some description of the reasons for referral should be reviewed. The child is invited to explain his/her understanding for the assessment but typically will provide some vague description or indicate that they do not know. Invite the child to ask the parent and encourage the parent to explain the concerns simply. Importantly, help ensure that the parent is not blaming or accusing but stating a concern and desire to help their child.

Ask the parents to describe their concerns and guard against vague general statements and conclusions. It is critically important to obtain a detailed history of the emotional or behavioral issues of concern. Parents will often provide the clinician with a conclusion – for example, the child is stubborn, defiant, or does not listen or some other conclusion about their child. Once the clinician has obtained the parents' description of their concerns regarding their child, it is essential to obtain specific examples of the behavior about which they are concerned. Simply stating that Johnny does not listen, or that he is defiant, offers no information that is of explanatory value.

Ask the parent to describe the context and what was happening prior to the specific concerning behavior, the parental behavior, such as telling Johnny to clean his room, followed by a description of Johnny's behavior and the parental reaction. This detailed step-by-step description of the sequence of events and the parental instructions to the child are essential elements in the proper diagnosis and understanding of the child's behavioral and emotional difficulties.

For example, Mrs. J. reports that Johnny does not listen to her. She tells him to go upstairs and to get ready for school; he must put his toys away, put on his clothes, wash his face, brush his teeth, and come downstairs. Ten minutes pass and Johnny is upstairs playing with his toys. Parent's interpretation: Johnny is defiant and won't listen.

However, there are several possible reasons for the behavior: (1) Johnny has forgotten what he was supposed to do, having a poor auditory memory he remembered only that he was supposed to go upstairs. (2) Johnny has an ADD and is easily distracted. (3) Johnny is defiant and chooses to disobey his parent's instructions. In formulating the proper diagnosis and treatment plan, it is essential that the possibility of language delay be considered, because if present and overlooked, effective intervention will be incomplete and ineffective.

In this example, helping the parent to break down instructions into simpler one-step commands can make an important difference. The possibility of an ADD needs also to be considered, but these are common co-occurring conditions, and consequently the child must be assessed for both.

Obtaining the Chief Concern and History

Daily Life Functional Enquiry
A careful *functional enquiry* requires obtaining information about the child's progress in numerous aspects of his/her daily life. This includes his/her progress academically, behaviorally, and socially at school and at home. Enquire about behavior and relationships with parents and siblings and behavior with regard to any chores and household routines, such as at meals, and the morning and bedtime routines, use of television and computers; ask about social behavior with friends after school, on weekends, and any organized activities involving athletics, music, crafts, and creative arts, or any other hobby or interest.

Ask the parent to provide you with detailed information about their child's behavior and performance in each of these areas. This will help provide a more complete picture of how the child is getting along in most aspects of daily life. This will also indicate in which areas the child is encountering difficulties and in which areas he or she is functioning well.

Through this process, the areas of competence and trouble are identified, and a more complete understanding of the nature of the child's problems can be formulated. For example, one parent complained that their 10-year-old son was arrogant, defiant, showed no respect, and was always fighting with them. Careful enquiry revealed that the conflicts arose only with regard to homework. This boy had been in a religious parochial school and had separate English and math classes 3 days a week after his parochial school finished. He was expected to do homework every day. Detailed enquiry revealed that conflict over homework occurred on those days the boy attended his English and math class, and seldom on the days did he not. Once the parents recognized that the conflicts were restricted to homework, their definition of the problem changed, the homework schedule was revised, and their attitude to the boy shifted.

The Child's Playmates

Reinterpreting and reframing detailed examples of the child's behavior are key steps in helping parents modify unhelpful attitudes and conclusions

As part of the assessment process, enquire about the child's friends and playmates; assess the kind of play in which the child engages, the age group with whom the child commonly plays, whether the child is engaged in group or team sports and activities, games with rules, cooperative play or parallel play or solitary play, for instance. This information will inform your understanding of the child and the nature of his/her problems; it helps build a picture of the child's social relationships, his/her developmental level, interests, and areas of challenge as well as opportunities.

Ask the parents and the child to describe his/her friends and playmates. To fully appreciate the quality of the child's social relationships, obtain detailed descriptions of the nature of play or activities in which the child and his/her friends engage. Ask the parent to describe what they themselves have witnessed; reports witnessed by others that they convey cannot usually be relied upon because they are often incomplete or presented with a biased point of view (the parent of another child reported that Johnny hit their son, for example). A parent may report that Johnny has lots of friends, but has no play dates, is never invited to birthday parties or sleepovers. Clearly something is amiss in this child's social sphere.

Parents may say that Johnny plays much better with younger children. He is uncomfortable with children his own age, but plays well with children who are in a grade or two below his. There may be several reasons for this: Johnny may want to control the play and can do so with younger children, Johnny may feel threatened by children his own age, but not with younger children.

Information on the child's playmates and interactions with peers offers diagnostically helpful information that can assist in treatment planning.

The parents of one 5-year-old boy were concerned because he did not listen to them, would wander aimlessly repeating catchphrases he had heard on television, and they were perplexed on how to deal with him and how to understand him.

> T.: *Does J. have any friends or playmates?*
> P.: *Yes, he does. He plays with several friends.*
> T.: *Can you describe this play?*
> P.: *He plays with his sister, who is 8 years old, and her friends.*
> T.: *Okay. What exactly does he do when he plays with them?*
> P.: *They play house.*
> T.: *What does he do when they play house?*
> P.: *He is the baby.*

The child's play mates, type of play, and role in the play reveal the child's developmental level and social competence

This example illustrates the importance of clarifying the specifics of the child's play and playmates. It is apparent from this example that the child is not able to engage in any form of collaborative play, or play with rules, he is simply there as an object that his sister and her playmates can react to as though he were a baby. Although this boy is chronologically 5 years old, the level of his play is more in keeping with a much younger child. A key therapeutic task was to help the parents adjust their understanding of his developmental level and recognize that he was functioning as a much younger child than his age would suggest.

In this example, the parents will need to be more hands-on with J., speak to him in shorter simpler language, use visual cues, and be more physically directive with him. He is less able to respond to oral instructions and will need to be shown or physically redirected more often than had previously been assumed.

Developmental History

Enquire about the child's birth and development: Was the pregnancy with this child full term, were there any problems during the pregnancy, any history of medications, smoking, drugs, or alcohol during the pregnancy? Was this a normal vaginal delivery, and were there any problems or complications with the child at the time of delivery? Ask about the child's developmental milestones, in particular the age at which the child spoke in single words, the age at which he/she spoke in two to three word phrases, and their assessment of his understanding of oral language even if his expressive language may have been somewhat delayed.

In addition to the child's language development, enquire about the child's gross and fine motor development and the age at which he walked, his ability to manipulate utensils, use of crayons, and play with toys, and so on. Here you want to discover if there is evidence of any perturbations in the child's developmental progress. For the clinical presentation in which you suspect LI, a careful developmental history with regard to language expression and comprehension and, to a lesser extent, fine motor development can be informative.

For the child who is attending school, be sure to ask about the child's progress academically with particular reference to reading. The child with delayed language development will be at high risk of reading delays (Beitchman & Young, 1997). When the information obtained suggests language and or reading delays, further clarification and confirmation by speech/language or psychoeducational assessment is required.

Clinical Pearl
Get Eyewitness Examples not Conclusions

Do not rely on vague general descriptions of the child's behavior problems. Obtain detailed first hand descriptions of the behavior of concern. Similarly, descriptions of the child's behavior with other children should be first-hand descriptions of what others have witnessed. This is important for several reasons: First, to be certain that you have a factual report of what transpired; second, that it has not been filtered with misinformation, misattribution, or bias; third, that you can discuss the parental understanding of the event and how they dealt with it; and fourth, this affords you an opportunity to engage the parent in a detailed exploration into the meaning of the child's behavior and steps they can take to address the concerns.

Family History

Obtaining a family history is a standard step in the assessment process. In taking a family history it is helpful to provide some context for the enquiry. Inform the parents that the kind of problems the child appears to have (e.g., delayed language development, anxiety, or attentional difficulties) tend to run in families, and it is informative to understand if there is a family history for any similar problems. Ask the parents about any family history of psychological or psychiatric disorders. Ask about first-degree biological relatives of both parents. Enquire about any history of language or learning difficulties. Listen for information that suggests a parental history of academic struggles, and the parental educational level and current job. This will provide some context of the child's difficulties and the degree to which it is similar to aspects of the parental history. While none of this information is by itself confirmatory, it does help contribute to the formulation and will be an important part of the feedback to the parents and the child.

The Interview With the Child (or Youth)

During the assessment process, the clinician has a relatively short period of time and may give more support if needed to elicit responses from the child. The clinician will need to be more patient and encouraging of the child's attempt to explain himself/herself; the clinician may need to repeat what the child has said and perhaps extend and elaborate the child's communicative intent, checking to be sure that the clinician has correctly understood the child's intended communication.

The interview with the child will include observations of the child's behavior with his/her parents, how he/she responds to their comments or directions. Do they seem to be following the conversation, or are they busily engaged playing with toys, coloring, or otherwise occupied? What is their understanding of the reason for the referral? Does he/she recognize having some difficulties? Commonly children will acknowledge that they get into trouble at school, that other kids bug them, or that their parents shout at them too much. Children may however reveal that they feel they are blamed for things they did not do or cannot control, or that other kids distract them, or that they do not understand why their parents are always so mad at them.

Giving the child an opportunity to be seen alone and to convey his/her concerns is an important part of formulating the treatment plan. This interview is also used to obtain an impression of the child's developmental level and language competence. Assessing the child's expressive language through conversing with the child will provide an initial impression, and if concerns regarding the child's language competence exist, formal testing should be arranged. Likewise, any suspicion that the child's receptive language or language comprehension is below age level will need to be formally assessed. The behavioral and emotional problems evident in the LI child are illustrated in Case Vignettes 2, 3, and 4.

Case Vignette 2
Problem With Staying on Task

Staying on topic is a commonly reported childhood problem. For example, a 10-year-old girl, when asked to retell a story, could not stay on topic:

G.: *They were building a house, and they had no place to live so they're going to find a house. And some people don't have a house, they live outside. But people live in a house.*

Q.: *What happened after they build the house?*

G.: *They were sad because it was thunderstorm ... (singing) la la la, I am walking to go to Bi Way because I love it. ... (the child is refocused on the task) 'cause they were sleeping and they were crying, they were sad. Anyways! (she laughs) I don't like this story.*

It is apparent that this girl has difficulty remaining on task. Although it is possible that the emotional content of the story affected her willingness and ability to tell the story, this difficulty is typical of children with ADDs. The manifest problem of topic maintenance may be due to underlying language problems such as poor auditory memory, attentional problems, or as is illustrated in this case, the emotional content of the story itself. Whatever the reason, these children have problems with storytelling, a task that taps skills that are central to one's ability to communicate.

Case Vignette 3
Behavioral Problems in a 4-Year-Old Girl With Language-Processing and Auditory Discrimination Difficulties

This case is that of a 4-year-old girl who was referred because of behavioral problems. The mother had complained that she and her daughter were in frequent conflict. The child did not follow the mother's requests, frequently had temper tantrums, would shout and call her mother names, and was often inconsolable and unreasonably obstinate.

If asked to complete a task, or to join other children in a group activity, she was prone to misunderstand the demand characteristics of the situation and stomp away in contemptuous disgust, saying that she hated the place, the school, and the people and would not comply with such stupid requests. For instance, on one occasion, the children in her play group had intended to play tea party, but S. stormed away shouting that she did not want a "tarpy." She heard the words *tea party* as "tarpy" and of course did not know what it was. S. had deficiencies of language processing. This included difficulties with auditory discrimination. Situations that would have been simple and straightforward for most children became frustrating and complex for her. She would react to the frustration with temper tantrums and rages.

Her attempts to achieve mastery and competence were continually met with surprises that confused her, frustrated her, and led to angry outbursts. She had difficulty participating with other children partly because she did not understand much of what transpired. Because of these problems, she often found herself ostracized and teased by other children and, consequently, sought to avoid them.

The understanding of this child's language-processing difficulties held significant implications for treatment approaches. The recognition of the language problems also helped dissipate the sense of willfulness and deliberate defiance commonly present when conflicts of this nature arise. It became possible to help the mother understand that the child's shouts, tantrums, and defiance were more a reaction to confusion and upset, than a willful attempt to hurt or defy her mother. This shifted the therapeutic focus, allowed the mother to try to understand her child and minimize the child's confusion. Oral communication with S. would need to be slower paced, with clear enunciation, and close attention to whether S. had understood what was being said.

The language deficits may not have been responsible for all her difficulties, but they contributed significantly, primarily by heightening this child's sensitivity to failure and narcissistic injury. This often showed itself in the form of oppositional behavior – behavior that was not simply intended as an angry negativistic repudiation, but rather as a self-preservative attempt at mastery and independence. Placed in this light, it became easier for the child's parents and the therapeutic team to help S. during these periods, by not taking it personally, by recognizing the behavior for what it was, and gently telling S. that it is okay to make mistakes, no one is perfect.

Case Vignette 3 illustrates ways in which difficulties in auditory discrimination contributed to the child's behavioral challenges.

In this case, simply recognizing that the child had auditory discrimination difficulties had an important therapeutic effect; it helped explain some of the child's outbursts, redefined the perception of the child as willful and oppositional, to that of a child who struggles to maintain self-esteem and a sense of competence despite serious challenges in understanding oral exchange.

Case Vignette 4
Language Disorder and Comorbid Anxiety

This is a transcript of a short interchange with an 8-year-old boy who had become highly anxious; the family were at a loss to understand this and sought help. The referring physician raised concerns that Freddy might be developing a thought disorder as a prelude to an emerging psychosis or possibly schizophrenia.

Freddy enters the play room:
Doctor (D.): *What do you suppose you would like to do today?*
F.: *I don't know.*
D.: *What things do you like to do?*
F.: (long pause) *I don't know what things I like to do.*
D.: *Do you like to watch television? ... Do you like to play with toys?*
F.: (long pause) *Well, I like to do a lot of things.* (Freddy is then invited to play with some of the figures and toys on the tabletop as he and the doctor sit on the floor together)
D.: *We'll put some of these things on the floor so you can play with them if you like. Would you like to do that?*
F.: *Yup.* (Freddy is moving blocks and various objects around)
D.: *There are lots of people over there, aren't there?*
F.: Identifies two small figures, saying, "*This is Dr. Y. He has bits of hair kind of like he is bald,*" referring to a hairless, plastic figure of a boy.
(begins to whisper) *Maybe you can have some time, I'm having appointment, I am a dentist appointment 'cus I have a cavity. I have to get filled in my head 'cus they are going to take some X-rays so I am going to have to use that now 'cus we never cured this before.*
D.: *Okay. Alright.*
F.: (begins to mumble) Invited to repeat what he said.
F.: *Taking a dentist appointment.*
D.: *You're taking a dentist appointment?*
F.: *Yup. He has a little cavity. I'm going to take it from him 'cus it's stuck there. 'Cus my humor is kind of silly for me. He sure doesn't like it, but he knows there is too far and so he was losing a lot of hair so he needs a new way. So I'm having this appointment. Um, I'll mention what that thing on the air. It's going to be up to my hair so they are going to take it 'cus it's already sucked in. Where they are going to put me to sleep with some magic pills and then I have to do is really put me to sleep and take out and there will be a hole and they are going to take it out and put a radio in and it'll lose all its energy and they'll chop off its head.*

Freddy had an appointment with a dentist, was told that he had a cavity that would need to be filled. He would receive an anesthetic. He was confused and terrified about what was going to happen to him but could not explain how he felt or why. Freddy had the idea that they were going to make a hole in his head or mouth and put a radio in it and maybe chop off his head!

As his conversation continued uninterrupted, it became progressively more disorganized and fantastical. His ideas were barely coherent, and he shifted between the first and third person – especially when discussing the scary stuff. Without knowing the context, Freddy could easily be considered to have a thought disorder and could be labeled "psychotic." But Freddy's difficulties are due to poor comprehension and expression and not a distortion in the perception of reality.

Children can acquire and develop these fanciful and fantastical ideas, and that does not mean they are psychotic or otherwise lying or malingering. His misunderstanding of the nature of the dental appointment increased his anxiety to the point that he feared they would chop off his head. In the vignette, he is so scared about what he imagines will happen at the dentist, that he displaces the act onto the toy figure – they "chop off its head." In this vignette, Freddy's difficulties with expressive language are evident in the lack of a coherent narrative and immature, incomplete sentences. His anxiety is driven by his confusion and poor comprehension of what was going to happen at the dentist's office.

In contrast to S. in Case Vignette 3, Freddy did not have tantrums, instead he would become anxious when he failed to understand events and circumstances and needed lots of reassurance. Additionally, Freddy is prone to suffer in silence; it is up to the adults in Freddy's life to recognize his upset and offer help. It is critically important that the adults in Freddy's life recognize that he would have difficulties with auditory comprehension and that consequently explaining events and circumstances to him would require greater planning and attention. Physical props, rehearsals, and careful, deliberate dialogue with Freddy to solicit feedback as to what he understands would be a requisite part of successful communications with him.

This is an example of a focused intervention around a defined event or episode. Once the reason for Freddy's anxiety is known, the nature of the dental visit can be explained to offer him reassurance and reduce his level of anxiety.

He will need ongoing therapy for his language delays (see below). There was no evidence that Freddy suffered from ongoing anxieties or an anxiety disorder; however, his parents were cognizant of the need to monitor his progress and were primed to seek assistance if Freddy's anxieties returned.

Giving Feedback

Giving feedback to the parents and child is the first step in the treatment plan. Successful treatment with children depends on establishing a strong therapeutic alliance with the child and the child's parents. Providing the results and feedback of the assessment is a critical step in preparing the family and the child for the therapeutic recommendations; it can be a make or break opportunity to establish a therapeutic alliance.

Once you have arrived at a diagnosis you must explain your understanding to the parents and to the child. Be careful to avoid conveying any sense of blame either of the child or the parents. Parents often feel guilty and responsible for their child's problems and will be sensitive to any hint that they are to blame. Additionally, many children will feel that they have been bad and feel singled out in a way that makes them uncomfortable. Explain that while the parents are not the cause of the child's behavioral or emotional problems, they are part of the solution. Likewise with the child, while he or she does not choose to have the behavioral and emotional problems, there are things they can do to make things better. Use this opportunity to help the parents understand the specific types of challenges the child faces using his/her own words and their examples and explain how the nature of the child's problems contributes to the child's behavioral difficulties. For instance, the child with delayed language development will have increased difficulties being flexible in his/her thinking and in being able to adapt to new and different situations easily. This is a developmental and therapeutic challenge.

Reading-disabled children may have trouble hearing sound blends such as /bl/. It is like being color blind for sounds

For the child with comorbid LI who has had speech and language testing or psychoeducational testing, plan joint feedback with the psychologist or speech/language pathologist. Arrange to meet before the feedback session with the parents to ensure that you and the psychologist or speech/language pathologist are in sync on the findings and the recommendations. Explain the importance of the delays or deficits and the impact that they are having on the child. For example, one family when told their child had a language-based learning disability in which the child had trouble hearing sound blends such as *ph* or *th* or *bl*, for instance, and consequently did not recognize them on the printed page, responded by indicating that it was as though the child was *color blind for sounds*. This was a succinct yet powerful conceptualization of the child's reading disability and helped the parents to become more supportive and less intolerant of their child's academic and behavioral struggles. Appendices 5 and 6 are handouts for parents. Appendix 5 contains some information on language impairment/delay, their associated psychosocial difficulties, and long-term outcomes. A number of online resources that offer additional information parents may find useful is found in Appendix 6.

Avoid offering generalizations; instead, tailor your comments to each particular case to convey your understanding and your recommendations. For example, one young 10-year-old boy with comorbid LI and anxiety, when describing some of his worries, explained that he was afraid to go outside because the man who did all the killing (in the Virginia Tech massacre) was still alive and he could still kill more people. This boy, who lived in Toronto, did not know that the massacre had occurred in Virginia. Instead he believed the shooter was still alive and living in Toronto.

In this example, the parents need to be vigilant about what their child watches on television, and should check in with him daily on any potential concerns and misinformation. This is especially true with the more inhibited, LI child, since communicating will be more effortful, and the child may be harboring unfounded fears that once exposed can be ameliorated.

Parental Issues

Be sure to arrive at an understanding of the parent's level of stress, the degree to which they are or can be in agreement on the concerns relating to their child and what needs to be done. For the situation in which the parents convey stress that seems disproportionate to the child's difficulties, determine whether there are other issues at play. The parents could be at odds on the approach to child rearing and discipline, there could be marital issues that are dividing the parents and contributing to the child's problems, there may be financial issues, etc. Nevertheless, even when there are marital issues contributing to the child's problems, you may need to offer the child some form of intervention. Failing to do so will affect your credibility with the parents and run the risk of alienating them. The intervention may involve helping the child cope with the parental conflict. If you are confident that the child is doing well and that the issues reside with the parents, you can offer to monitor the child's progress in response to their participation in therapy.

In one case, the parents were insistent that the school was not handling their child's learning and behavior problems properly. Even though the child had had an individual education plan in place, and the school reported that they were implementing the plan, the family continued to insist that the school was not doing enough and held the school responsible for the child's behavioral difficulties. Only after the parents were convinced that the therapeutic team took the family's concerns seriously and developed a trusting relationship, did the full extent of the parental conflict become evident. The long-standing ongoing marital dispute that contributed to their child's behavior problems was largely inaccessible until sufficient trust had been established.

Clinical Pearl
How to Ask About Emotional Climate at Home

Sometimes challenging situations arise in which the parental attitude suggests resistance to questions about themselves and their marital relationship, preferring to keep the focus on their child. Here is one way to approach parents to address these issues: Concerns about Johnny (or Mary) can be worrisome and stressful.

T.: *How have you been coping with these concerns?*

You can follow up by asking about the strategies they have used to deal with the problems with Johnny, how it is working and whether both parents agree on the approach. This then opens up the parental approach to parenting and differences and conflicts will become evident. It is relatively straightforward to then ask whether the concerns about parenting and the worries about Johnny have affected how they are getting along.

T.: *I see that you each have different ideas on how to help Johnny. How do you solve these differences?*

P.: *We have not been able to do so.*

T.: *Has not being able to agree on what to do affected how you are getting along?*

Often one of the parents will then volunteer that they have differences in other aspects of their relationship. The point of this enquiry is to obtain a sense of the emotional climate in the home, what impact it is having on the child, and whether it needs to be a focus of therapy.

When talking with the parents about their child's behavioral and emotional problems, ask the parents how the concerns about their child has affected them, how they are coping, and whether it has led to conflicts between them.

Acknowledge that it is understandable that they would feel stressed since, among other things, it indicates their care and concern for their child. When parental stress is an ongoing issue, engage the parents in discussions regarding their need for therapy or support for their own concerns, independent of their child. Reducing the level of stress and tension in the home setting will help lower the temperature at home and should result in improvements in the child's behavioral and emotional functioning.

Differentiating Parental Issues From the Child's Issues

Be alert to the parent who confuses timelines. For instance, one parent complained about their child smearing feces, having tantrums, and refusing to follow parental direction. On further enquiry, the parent recognized this behavior occurred when the child was a preschooler and not now that the child was 9 years old. Nevertheless the parent insisted that they continued to have many problems with the child's behavior but could offer no specific examples. To help clarify and identify the issues of concern, the parent was asked to keep a diary of the behavioral issues that arose over the next 2 weeks. When seen 2 weeks later, the parent sheepishly realized that there had not been any behavioral issues involving the child during the preceding 2 weeks. In this instance, the real issue driving the parental concerns involved the marital relationship.

Occasionally parents will present with concerns about their child that seem out of proportion to the child's presentation. A parent who is depressed or is experiencing chronic stress may find the relentless demands of looking after their child overwhelming and will reframe the child's normative behavior as pathological, or fail to recognize that some of the child's behavior is in reaction to the parent's depression, for example. In this case, it is important to be alert to the state of mind of the parent and to ensure that the parent is offered appropriate support, while clarifying the nature of the child's problem if any is present. Additionally, in some instances, parental concerns arise because they do not understand developmentally appropriate behavior and misjudge their child's normative behavior as problematic.

Case Vignette 5
Pathologizing Normative Behavior

One 10-year-old boy Seth had been referred for an assessment because of concerns regarding memory problems. He had been seen by his family doctor, referred to a neurologist who conducted an EEG and CAT scan, and could not identify the reason for the memory problem.

During the course of the psychiatric assessment, the parent was asked to give an example of Seth's memory problem, she replied that when she asked Seth to take out the garbage, he would say he would, but when the time came he would forget. She was unable to offer any examples of memory problems that could not be understood as normative behavior. There were no academic issues, and the boy was progressing normally at school.

In talking with Seth, he agreed that he did sometimes forget to take out the garbage, but mostly he was in a hurry to get to school so he could play with his friends.

In this example, in addition to a very poor understanding of this normative behavior, the mother was under considerable stress. She was a single mother, struggling financially to make ends meet, while trying to support an increasingly challenging elder parent. In this example, helping the mother contend with her many challenges, while educating her on the normative behavior of her son represented a first step in the therapeutic process.

Discussing Family History

At the time you are providing feedback, you will have specific details about the parental history that can be helpful in explaining the child's problems to the parents. This information can help the parents understand their child's difficulties and to be supportive. A parent may say, "I was just like him when I was a child but we did not know what it was back then." Occasionally parents will be in disagreement on the need for an assessment or treatment. Father may say that he was just like Johnny, and he turned out okay, whereas mother will be concerned because she has received complaints from school that Johnny is not doing his work, or that he gets into trouble. Both parents need to be involved in discussing these issues.

Occasionally a parent will be concerned that their son or daughter will develop the same problems as an uncle or aunt or cousin who is described as a ne'er do well or drug addict or worse. Use this opportunity to explain the nature of the child's problems and the role they can play in preventing the outcome they fear. Parental motivation for treatment engagement will be high.

Clinical Pearl
Taming the Internet

With the wide availability of the Internet, parents will scour it in an attempt to diagnose their child's problems. This generates considerable misinformation and anxiety.

Review the parents' Internet information; clarify and correct their information and interpretation, then describe your diagnosis, recommendations, and prognosis. Help the parents recognize that they have wrongly identified some behavior as symptomatic of a feared diagnosis when in fact the behavior is in response to a particular event and does not signify any specific diagnosis. This will help reduce their level of anxiety about their child.

4.1.4 Organizing the Treatment

Once you have given the parents and the child feedback from your assessment they will want to know what can be done to help their child. For the child with anxiety and comorbid LI, treatment is multitiered and can proceed along three parallel paths. (1) Treatment specifically directed at the speech and or language delay would constitute one path. This form of treatment will usually be provided by, in collaboration with, or under the direction of a speech/language pathologist and will be focused on the child's specific difficulty; this would have been discussed at the time of the feedback but may need to be reviewed again. The focus could be phonological processing, vocabulary, grammatical structures, comprehension, and memory, for example. (2) The second path would involve attention to any concurrent psychological, emotional, and behavioral concerns and would include some form of individual psychotherapy. (3) The third path would involve modifying the child's environment to promote growth and reduce emotional and behavioral problems. This usually involves working with the school and the parents. It may be helpful to include others, such as a coach or scout leader, for instance, but these issues will be decided later and will be case specific. Encouraging the child to join an organized group activity to supplement individual therapy is often advisable, but ultimately depends on whether these group activities are available and affordable, and whether, in the judgment of the family and clinician, they are desirable experiences for the child. Of course the child would need to be willing to attend these group activities. If initially the child declines to be enrolled, this could then become a therapeutic target of the work with the child.

You will need to describe the approach to therapy that you are recommending, what it will consist of, for how long, how often, and for what period of time. Explain that you will be meeting alone with Johnny for about 45 min once a week for X number of weeks. The number of weeks will vary depending on the particular disorder and its severity. Inform the parents and the child that you will also meet with the parents periodically to be sure that you are all working together as a team. Organize your office so that you have the same materials present at each session and be sure to prepare a locker or file drawer where you keep Johnny's material. This may consist of Johnny's workbooks that you are doing together, it may also contain drawings or play materials that are specific to the work with Johnny.

Depending on the case particulars, you may need to work with Johnny's school. This is likely to be true in those instances in which problems have been identified at school. Check that the parents are comfortable with having you contact the school. Review with the parents and with Johnny the specific plan that involves the school. Contacting the school can be staged so that there is an initial period of individual work before the school is involved as a therapeutic partner.

It will be necessary to work with Johnny's parents but the degree to which it is necessary and the type of work will depend on the role they can play in ameliorating Johnny's difficulties. Where there is a history of parent–child conflict, work with the parents will be an important part of the overall therapeutic process. Where the issues are localized to anxieties at school, work with the parents can be less frequent and more supportive of the therapy with the child.

You have provided feedback to the parents and the child, you have described the therapy recommendations, and the parents and child have agreed. You are ready to begin the therapy.

Strengths-Based Approaches

Traditionally the diagnostic process is intended to assess symptoms, concerns, clarify areas of deficit, and arrive at a formulation; the results of the assessment form the basis upon which intervention is organized and implemented. There is, however, growing recognition of the importance of assessing the strengths of the child and family and incorporating them into the overall intervention plan. A strength-based assessment measures those emotional and behavioral skills, competencies, etc. that create a sense of personal accomplishment and contribute to satisfying relationships with family members, peers, adults, and others. They enhance one's ability to deal with adversity and stress and promote one's personal, social, and academic development (Epstein & Sharma, 1998).

There are many different kinds of strengths that can be drawn upon and diverse ways to describe them. Some focus upon personal strengths, such as social competence, problem solving, autonomy, and sense of purpose (Ellis, 2011). Some assessment tools have been developed that provide an overall strength index, with summary strengths in five areas: interpersonal strength, (ability to interact with others), the child's relationship with his/her family, the child's perception of his/her competence and accomplishments, the child's competence/ performance in the classroom, and the child's ability to give and receive affection from others (Buckley & Epstein, 2004).

Attention to these strengths provides opportunities for the child and family to progress in ways that contribute to their sense of well-being and success, even if the specific symptoms or deficit that brought them to seek help has not been entirely resolved. Including a strength-based approach supports hope and resilience, and promotes healthy growth and development that serve as a counterweight to the symptoms and concerns that prompted the assessment. It is an important bridge to establishing the alliance with the child and family.

Establishing the Alliance

Incorporating a strength-based approach helps the child and family recognize that you are aware of their many strengths and abilities, conveys hope and respect and that you see the child or youth as a whole person and not just someone with symptoms and a diagnosis. This helps set the stage to negotiate the treatment alliance.

The motivation to pursue therapy will be different for the anxious child compared with the child with a DBD. The anxious child may want to reduce his or her level of anxiety but may not be enthusiastic about some of the therapeutic tasks to achieve that end. Children with a DBD diagnosis do not usually recognize their contribution to the problem and may more commonly see themselves as a victim or as helpless to do anything about the problem. The parents and school are usually driving the need for the intervention. Because these different conditions require different approaches, we will consider them separately.

The initial task is to ensure that the child feels safe and comfortable with the therapist. Typically, the child will get his/her cues from his parents who demonstrate their acceptance of, and respect for, the therapist and the therapeutic process. The parents and therapist together speak with the child identifying his/her worries and anxieties and that seeing the therapist will be a way to turn the big worries into little ones and eventually make them go away. This begins the process by which the therapist and child identify the different worries the child has. In establishing the alliance with the child, it is usually best to combine some element of light fun, such as with a game or toy, and some focused work on the child's particular problem. Tell the child that some of your work together may involve some play materials, such as a game or play figures, for instance. In your work with the child you will need to convey empathy and respect for the child, yet maintain a developmentally appropriate tone – for instance, using words and language that is geared to the child's developmental level. If utilizing a CBT approach, explain the process to the child and the importance of practicing at home. It is usually better not to use the term *homework* since it may turn off some children.

Parental involvement and the parental attitude can be critical. The parent may feel helpless to address the child's social anxieties. The parent may fluctuate between, on the one hand, accepting the child's reluctance to tackle some of his/her fears, versus on the other hand, encouraging the child to face them, thereby conveying an attitude that the child will be able to master the fear. Engaging the parents in the therapeutic process, educating them about the nature of the child's problems and the therapy, and conveying hope represent key elements for a successful intervention.

For parents who may be suffering from anxiety, or struggling financially, or have language and communication problems themselves, helping their child can represent formidable challenges. Attending to the parental issues and supporting them through this process can be a key ingredient in moving the case forward.

For the pre-pubertal child you will need to maintain regular face-to-face contact with the parents, meeting at some regular interval or intermixing phone contact with face-to-face contact. Regular contact with the parents of a teenager is important to ensure continued parental support, but the youth will need to be reassured about issues of confidentiality and may want to attend joint sessions. Feedback with the parents can take the form of indicating their son or daughter is attending regularly and that progress is being made. However, the parents may need more support than occasional feedback, in which case the parents may need to be seen by a colleague, to maintain a clear separation between the individual work with the youth and the work with the parents.

Clinical Pearl
Avoid Unholy Contracts

Avoid overidentifying with the parents or the child. Sometimes the therapist will get into an unrecognized and implicit contract with the parent that they will "fix" their child. A situation can then arise in which the parent complains to the therapist that the child's behavior has gotten worse; sending a strong message that the therapist has not done enough to improve the child's behavior. Alarm bells should go off; avoid the danger of acting as an agent for the parent and untherapeutically challenging the child on his/her behavior. Before you can address any of these issues with the child, you will need to carefully reframe the alliance with the parent, acknowledge their frustration, and educate them on the process of therapy, what can realistically be expected, and what your role is vis-à-vis the child and the parent. It may then be appropriate to arrange a joint meeting with the parent and the child to review the issues at hand.

Focus on Emotional Issues

CBT is considered the standard approach to the treatment of anxiety disorders (Rapee, Schniering, & Hudson, 2009). Here we outline some of the standard techniques utilized and the modifications in these techniques for use with children with comorbid language delays. Once it is established that the child will participate in therapy, the child is helped to identify and articulate the specific fear or worry, and then an approach to dealing with it is developed. A majority of the fears and worries involve social and interpersonal relations.

Although you will have obtained a detailed history at the time of the initial assessment, the initial stages of therapy require that you obtain precise information of the situations in which the child is anxious. This allows you to identify the specific situations and the targets that will be the focus of the interventions. Because of the child's language delays, he/she is vulnerable to anxiety in several different ways. For example, the children's expressive language may single them out as less mature than their age mates, and they will be subject to teasing and ridicule. Delays in auditory comprehension or memory will interfere with their ability to participate fully in the ongoing discussions among their peers, and they may appear to be out of step with the discussion and be subject to teasing and ridicule for comments that seem inappropriate to the discussion at hand.

Consequently, obtaining a detailed inventory of the situations in which the child experiences anxiety is a necessary first step. School and academics are common sources of anxiety and are a good place to start. Get as detailed a picture as possible of the situations in which the child feels anxious.

Here are some situations in which children experience anxiety:
- Anxiety about going to school;
- Anxiety about speaking in front of the class;
- Anxiety during recess because they will have no one with whom to play;
- Anxiety during lunch because they won't have anyone to sit with;
- Anxiety about failing the academic subjects;
- Anxiety that the teacher will be angry or critical;
- Anxiety about peers teasing or otherwise being mean or unfriendly.

These anxieties also present with certain variations, for example, anxiety about being teased may also include anxiety about wearing the "right" clothes, or rooting for the wrong team, etc.

Focus on Social and Interpersonal Problems

Social problems are common. These children may be socially ostracized, remaining on the periphery of their peer group, and unable to join in their play or activities. Organized groups targeting skills and activities in which the child is comfortable is an important step toward helping him/her gain confidence in the social milieu. Recess and lunchtimes can be especially stressful for the child who has been excluded from his/her peer group. School personnel need to be alert to children who remain on the periphery, frozen in their anxiety. These children need help to feel accepted and that they belong. Schools can organize special staff-led groups that include children selected to facilitate integrating these anxious language-delayed children into the group.

In parallel with these approaches, individual sessions with the child should focus on recognizing the triggers, identifying the emotions, and developing strategies to self-regulate and to acquire the skills to neutralize these anxieties. Ordinarily this will entail greater use of play materials, props, and pictures; dramatic reenacting of situations past and anticipated are useful approaches with language-delayed children.

The principles of CBT apply here, with the provision that modifications in the specific techniques utilized (e.g., how much written homework and how

Elements of Sucessful Treatment

The best results will be obtained with treatment that encompasses several key elements:

(1) Work closely with the parents; they are often key to successful intervention.

(2) Work with the child's teacher and school personnel to support the therapeutic approach.

(3) Work with the child. This can encompass:
   (a) Individual therapy, commonly based on CBT principles.
   (b) Social skills training to develop social skills.
   (c) General assistance to enhance communicative competence with discourse skills.
   (d) Help the child identify and build upon areas of strength and competence.

much role play), given the child's language delay, will be required. These modifications (described earlier) need to be titrated depending on the severity of the child's anxiety disorder and the language delay.

Work With the Parents

Remind the parents to encourage the child to participate fully in the therapy. This need not be an explicit directive, but can emerge in the context of a conversation with the parents when they are asked about Johnny's response to the therapy for instance. Parents can help by talking about the process of therapy and some of the issues that they themselves may have faced and overcome. They will need to support the child's efforts to face some of the situations and activities that they fear. They can act as a sounding board; provide opportunities for role play and rehearsal. To the extent that they are aware of situations that contribute to the child's anxieties and can do something about them, they should eliminate them (watching the news, for example). Watching news reports of killings, assaults, or thefts will contribute to the child's anxieties that the world is a dangerous place. Typically the child will have difficulty recognizing that within their own neighborhood these events are rare; furthermore, most young children will have trouble understanding geographic distances, so that a news report of an incident in another state or country can easily be assumed to be next door. Parents can reframe some of the child's misinterpretation of events. If watching a news report of an untoward incident, put the incident in context, noting the location and the rarity of the event as a way of reassuring the child that they need not worry about the event described in the news cast.

Work With the School

Work with school personnel to structure the child's school experience to minimize his/her anxiety. Here the idea is for school personnel to modify certain expectations that have been identified as creating/contributing to child's anxiety. Schools can adopt a wide variety of techniques to assist these children. The child can have a practice run with the teacher prior to presenting to the class. The format and expectations of the presentation can be adjusted to accommodate the child's needs – for example, with greater use of graphs or pictures, or other prompts to help the child perform in front of the class. Practicing and rehearsing an oral presentation prior to delivering it in class, and preparing visual and concrete aids to assist the child in presenting in front of his/her class can all be helpful. Adjust expectations to be consistent with the child's ability and titrate the expectations upwards with the child's progress.

Work With the Child

The therapeutic work with the child will encompass several different elements depending on the individual child: CBT is the underlying basic strategy. In addition, other elements include: social skills, communicative competence, and building on strengths. These are outlined below:

(1) Work with the child to help him/her acquire the skills and ability to self-regulate his/her anxiety. This is the process of CBT. The child is helped to identify and label emotions, and to parse them to more accurately reflect the intensity and valence of the affect. Through this process, the child gradually acquires a greater understanding of his/her emotional reactions. The next step is to define and articulate the triggers or situations and the emotional reactions these generate. This allows the child to develop strategies to prevent or reduce the anxiety. Developing techniques of self-talk and relaxation are additional ways to help prevent and reduce anxiety. For example, recognizing that some fears are unrealistic or highly improbable, the child is encouraged to prompt him/herself to consider the more probable safe alternative.

(2) Social skills: Work with the child to enhance knowledge and skills to build confidence in dealing with the anxiety-provoking situations. Here the plan is to teach the child strategies that may be used to help gain entry to a peer play group. For instance, a stepwise process can be used to guide the child: namely, observe, approach and gain eye contact, and ask "Can I play with you?" or "Can I play too?" If the child has a toy or some suitable play object, this may facilitate entry.

(3) Communicative competence: General assistance to enhance communicative competence with discourse skills may be part of the intervention. Skills that include topic maintenance, turn taking, requesting, commenting, narratives, and responding, once acquired can assist the child in forging connections with peers (Gallagher, 1999).

(4) Building on strengths: An important component in the work with the child is to identify areas of strength and competence. This could be athletics, music, arts and crafts – any area in which the child shows some interest, skill, or aptitude will be an important focus around which to build self-esteem, confidence, and ultimately friendships, social relationships, and feelings of success. This will also serve as a vehicle to develop friendships. Friendships arise out of shared interests, and participating in group activities such as soccer; or individual athletics such as gymnastics, music, or crafts, etc. can lead to friends with similar interests. The child will be interacting with other children who share those similar interests. Through this process the child can develop friendships that would carry over to the school.

Focus on Attentional Problems and Disruptive Behavior

Treatment for the ADHD child with comorbid language delays will incorporate most of the same elements utilized with the ADHD child but with modifications for the LI. These include parent training, working with the school, individual CBT/behavioral approaches, and the possible use of medication.

The child presenting with ADHD symptoms should be presumed to have LI or a learning disability unless proven otherwise

ADHD is one of the most common childhood psychiatric disorders and is highly comorbid with learning disabilities. It is therefore another important route by which a children may present with undiagnosed LI. The inattentive form of ADD has been associated with subpar academic progress in children who appear quiet and well behaved in a classroom setting and consequently do not come to the attention of special education resources until it is apparent that the child has been falling behind academically. In all of these instances, the child or adolescent should be presumed to have learning difficulties and unless proven otherwise a learning disability. Any child presenting with symptoms consistent with ADHD must be assessed with regard to his/her academic progress and the possibility of a learning disability, not only because they are commonly comorbid but because learning disabilities can be misinterpreted as attention problems and contribute to behavioral difficulties in the classroom setting.

Until proven otherwise, it is best to assume some degree of language and or learning delay. In working with the LI child with comorbid ADHD/ADD, several common elements of evidence-based treatment are described below. Some of these are mediated by the child's parents and teachers; others apply directly to the child. In delivering interventions based on these principles, the child's language capabilities need always to be considered.

Because it is almost always the parent or teacher who initiates the referral for the child with comorbid language delay and ADHD, you will need to obtain a detailed description from the parents and/or teacher of the situations in which the child shows symptoms. Meet separately with the parents to obtain a detailed description of the situations causing concern. Certain situations commonly recur and require a detailed examination of the issues involved. The child may recognize that their teacher or their parents have been admonishing them or punishing them, and they may feel that they are bad, or that it is not their fault but that they are being blamed for things they did not do or cannot control. Make note of the child's feelings and attitudes regarding the referral and the problems identified by the parents.

As in the case of the child with comorbid anxiety disorder and LI, a detailed functional enquiry of the situations and circumstances that are problematic for the child needs to be obtained. The first step is to obtain a careful history of the concerns regarding the child. Ask about the onset of the problem behavior and the circumstances in which they occur. Distinguish between problems reported at school, those reported at home, and those in the community.

Identifying the triggers and antecedent conditions that result in behavioral problems offers direction on the specific approach to treatment. Commonly, successful intervention will require a range of approaches, including those focused on the child's environment, work with the parents and teachers, and work directly with the child.

A history of delayed milestones for language acquisition supports the diagnosis of LI

A careful developmental history can be informative, with evidence that Johnny was late speaking in sentences and was difficult to understand beyond his fourth birthday, for example. Likewise, family history can be helpful. Is there any family history of language delays or learning difficulties? The father may acknowledge that he had very similar problems to ones Johnny seems to be having. Confirm the child's birth date and that the problems identified are not because Johnny is almost a full year younger than his classmates.

Teacher reports of the child's progress with reading will be informative and may confirm what has already been suspected, or alternatively raise questions on the need for further clarification.

Misjudging the child's developmental level will lead to frustration and failure. Consequently, expectations tailored to the child's developmental level, competencies, and language capabilities provide the framework within which the intervention is structured. You will need to help the parents adjust their expectations to be developmentally appropriate. This can be challenging.

One young 8-year-old told her therapist that she wanted to die so that she would no longer be a burden on her mother. In discussing this issue with the mother and reviewing some of issues involving her daughter, the therapist found that discrepancies between the mother's expectations of the child and what would ordinarily be considered appropriate mother–child expectations in their morning routine. Suzy was expected to get and make her own breakfast.

An 8-year-old may occasionally get or make her own breakfast, but preparing breakfast is a foundational parental responsibility and one that conveys caring, nurturing, and protection of the child. In the example given, there is an obvious rift in the mother–child relationship, and part of the problem was the mother's unrealistic expectations of her 8-year-old daughter.

Clinical Pearl
Empathy Melts Resistance

When the assessment indicates problems in the parent–child relationship, therapy may require changes by the child as well as the parent. When parents believe that they are doing everything they can to help Mary (or Johnny) but that Mary is not cooperating, they will expect you to "change" or "fix" Mary. How Mary is supposed to change becomes part of the therapeutic dialogue, but one important step is to help parents shift their attitude and approach. Before you can ask the parents to change their attitude or approach, you must avoid any suggestion of blame or criticism and convey empathy for their predicament. Acknowledge the parental efforts, acknowledge their pain and upset, and that despite all they do, the child shows little appreciation and "refuses" to respond to their efforts. Remind the parents that for most typically developing children, their approach would have been okay, but Mary has certain special needs (language impaired and ADHD, for example), so that their approach must be different. Now you can help articulate changes in the way the parents approach their child.

The initial steps in organizing treatment include an appreciation of the parent's feelings and attitudes toward their child. The parent may be feeling frustrated and angry because of their child, seeing him as deliberately misbehaving; there may be conflicts between parents on the approach to the child; they may feel under pressure because the school has been complaining and threatening to suspend him. They may be perplexed, and feel discouraged and depressed because of their challenges with their child. Before the specifics of treatment can be implemented you will need to understand and address the parental feelings and attitudes.

The first step in this process is to check their understanding of their child's difficulties, and their understanding of ADHD with LI, correcting any misunderstanding and misinformation. Explain the nature of ADHD with concomitant language delays. Although the specific etiology of ADHD is not known, much is known about the symptom picture, course, and response to interventions (Molina et al., 2009; Smith, 2010). Review the current understanding of ADHD, noting that ADHD is heterogeneous and may encompass many different kind of symptoms, but the most common ones (as they apply to their child) are problems with inhibitory control, sustaining attention, and completing tasks. The ADHD child will have problems with time perception and planning ahead to future events, being more focused on "the now."

Here it is important to explain that their child does not necessarily misbehave on purpose, and to a large extent his/her symptoms are a product of his/her environment and developmental level in certain key domains, as outlined earlier. The parents will need some reassurance that their child's condition is treatable, and that he/she can make progress. Inform the parents on the natural course, noting that some challenges may continue long term, but most symptoms can be expected to improve, and that with the treatment you will be recommending, they can be hopeful of more general progress.

Children do not choose to misbehave; they have not yet acquired the ability to control their impulses

Understanding these deficits will be an important part of organizing and implementing and treatment; it provides the framework for the child's treatment. The parents need to recognize that the child does not choose to be disinhibited but responds impulsively to situations because he/she has not yet acquired the ability to control his/her impulses. This has direct implications for the way some situations are organized – for instance, she may be asked not to touch dessert until she has finished her milk, but if the dessert is on the table in front of her, she will not be able to resist the impulse to reach for the dessert. Similarly, the ADHD child will be easily distracted, and consequently this needs to be factored into the parent's expectations of the child's behavior and performance in situations where there are distractions.

For the ADHD child with comorbid LI speak in short simple statements and repeat

For the child with ADHD and a comorbid language delay, these issues will be more challenging; extra steps will need to be taken to ensure the child understands what he/she has been told. Instructions, explanations, and directions will need to be delivered as short, simple statements, frequently checking with the child to be sure they follow and understand. Because of the concomitant language delays, the child will have difficulties explaining his/her ideas and concerns and will be at greater risk to feel frustrated and treated unfairly. Advise the parents or other relevant adult to calmly, quietly, and patiently help the child express his/her concerns so they can be redressed or some other action taken that achieves a satisfactory resolution.

Some Specific Areas of Difficulty

Homework. Completing homework is one of the most common battlegrounds between parents and children. Parents will commonly complain that "Johnny could do his homework in 10 minutes if he sat down to do it, instead we have to fight with him for an hour till he gets his homework done."

Until it is proven otherwise, assume the child may be language delayed and have a learning disability interfering with reading and reading compression. Remember that what may seem like a relatively simple bit of homework may be the adult equivalent of reading the fine print in an insurance contract or solving complex algebraic formulas!

Battling over homework is seldom helpful for the child or the parents, and steps need to be taken to interrupt this cycle. Unless there is strong evidence that there are no grounds to suspect language delay or a learning disability, psychoeducational testing is an important next step in guiding the approach to homework and academics more generally.

Battles about homework typically arise because parents worry that their child may not be progressing well enough academically. If this is a legitimate concern, the child will need to have psychoeducational testing. This will indicate whether he/she is working at the expected level or has a learning disability and needs an individual education plan. Once this information is available, the child's teacher can help articulate clear guidelines on home-work, and the parents together with the child should develop a homework plan. Homework should be done in the same location each time, in a quiet place with a minimum of distractions, and at the same time each day, with a minimum and sometimes a maximum amount of time dedicated to the home-work. The parents can offer an incentive if the child demonstrates progress academically, or completes the homework assignments consistent with the agreed-upon plan. The incentives can be for both short-term progress and for longer term progress.

Morning Routines. This is a common battleground, especially for parents who are working outside the home and must leave early. Young children will not understand the time pressure that parents feel, and rather than getting dressed, brushing their teeth, and attending to morning routines, the child may become distracted or dawdle instead, which leads to battles between the parent and child. This child might be described as dreamy, disorganized, defiant, and inattentive and unable to focus. Although there are no magic bullets that will transform the morning routine from one that is stressful and chaotic, to one that functions like that of a well-functioning team, there are some opportunities for improvement. For instance, simple changes in routines can be helpful. Helping the child prepare his/her clothes for school the evening before can reduce the task demands that may be experienced as overwhelming when they must be accomplished under time pressure just before leaving for school. Attention to these details may reveal other simple changes that will lessen the morning burden and reduce the morning stress.

Young children do not understand parental pressure to be ready on time

Ecological Approaches
Careful analysis of the situations in which the child experiences difficulties will identify opportunities to make changes to the physical setup and/or to the routines that are currently in place. For example, the child with ADHD should be placed near the front of the classroom as close to the teacher as possible and as far away from known distractions, such as a group of noisy classmates. The child's bedroom or play area should be structured to avoid overstimulating and overwhelming the child with too many choices and too many exciting things to

do or play with. Selecting a finite number of toys or games that are accessible helps the child better manage his play time.

4.1.5   Core Therapeutic Approaches

Below we describe some core therapeutic strategies that should be part of the therapist's tool bag. Not all of these approaches need be used with every child, nor should all of the same approaches necessarily be used with all children who have the same diagnostic issues. The specific approach utilized will depend upon a variety of factors, such as the age of the child, the specific profile of strengths and difficulties, and the relationship between the child and family.

Affect Education: Recognizing and Expressing Emotions

> **Children with LI have trouble recognizing, naming, and expressing their emotions. Help them attend to and label bodily sensations**

A key developmental step is the ability to recognize and label one's emotions and to express them in words. Difficulties recognizing and expressing emotions is a common issue in therapy with the LI child. It follows then that one of the first principles is to help the child and adolescent recognize their emotions. They will need to learn to attend to their bodily sensations, such as butterflies in the belly, or shaky or sweaty hands, rapid heartbeat, dizziness, light headedness, or intensely angry feelings. These feelings will need to be identified and labeled, with the child using the correct vocabulary to describe his/her emotions. Progress in recognizing their own emotions will contribute to progress in relationship building and interpersonal problem solving (see Appendix 7 for a handout for parents on practicing recognizing and processing emotions with their child).

Start with teaching single feelings with a developmental hierarchy of primary emotions such as happy, sad, scared, and mad. Later in the therapy, you can progress to more sophisticated or complex emotions such as empathy, sympathy, guilt, shame, envy, regret, etc. A variety of strategies can be utilized to assist the child in learning to recognize his/her emotions.

Show the child pictures of blank cartoon faces and ask the child to draw a happy, sad, mad, and scared face. You may need to model these facial expressions if the child is having trouble with this exercise. Use naturally occurring situations and draw the child's attention to facial and other features of emotional expression, labeling them, and modeling the language to express or illustrate those feelings. Role-playing activities can be scripted to teach language and expressiveness; stories from books, TV shows, and movies all provide excellent stimuli to assist children in formulating and expressing their emotions. Demonstrating or acting emotions out with the therapist can be helpful. Encouraging children to tell stories about their personal experiences helps them develop integrated language skills. For some children, a "feelings book" to draw and illustrate their emotions is a useful adjunct to the therapeutic work.

Connecting feelings with events: Not understanding what one is feeling and not knowing why one feels that way can be debilitating. Once the child begins to recognize internal states, the next step is to learn to connect these various feelings with events. For instance, not being invited to a friend's birthday party may evoke feelings of sadness, low self-esteem, and feelings of inadequacy.

Once the child is able to recognize and label these feelings, it is then possible to attribute them to the specific event and to engage the child in the process of therapy. For example, *"there can be many reasons that you were not invited that have nothing to do with you, such as only family members were invited,"* etc. This exchange provides the opportunity to help the child change his/her interpretation and alters his/her focus on self-blame and self-criticism.

The LI child will need more time to recognize and identify his/her feelings. You can use puppets to act out feelings and emotions to teach children to identify their feelings. For instance, a scenario can be played with puppets in which the mother wanders off, and the child is frightened that the mother has been lost or hurt. Invite the child to show you (with a face card) or tell you what the puppet child might be feeling. Various scenarios to illustrate other feelings can be enacted to give the child practice in identifying feelings. Puppet figures need not be people, farm or domestic animals such as horses, dogs, and cats work just as well, and for the younger child may work better.

Using puppets or small action figures of animals or humans helps the child express his/her feelings and emotions

For the LI child with ADHD / DBD, the focus is more likely to be on anger or upset that result in a meltdown. Tracking these situations will usually require cooperation between the child and parents, since it is likely that you will need input from both the parents and the child to piece together an accurate accounting of the sequence of events.

Example: After school one day, 9-year-old Scott was waiting in his mother's classroom (she was a teacher at his school) while she completed some of her work. Scott's home room teacher came into the classroom and, on seeing Scott, "told" him to help clean up the desks in their own classroom. Scott became very upset, shouting, crying, and carrying on for several minutes until he finally settled down.

In this example, Scott felt that his teacher was going to make him help clean up the classroom, but since it was after school, and he had already been dismissed he wanted to continuing playing while waiting for his mother. The task here is to help Scott identify his feelings and his thoughts: *this was unfair, this makes me mad, I don't need to do this, it is after school, and I want to play.* The home room teacher was not actually requiring Scott to help clean up, but instead was asking in the belief that Scott might have enjoyed assisting her. Reviewing the feelings and the thoughts with Scott and practicing alternate responses provides an opportunity to gain mastery of these situations. For instance, a thought bubble might be constructed for Scott: *"Having to clean up the classroom makes me upset, it is after school now and I don't need to do it, I would rather play."* The teacher's thought bubble would be *"Okay, Scott, I was only asking because I thought you would like to do it."*

Once children make progress in recognizing their own emotions, they are ready to acquire skills in recognizing the emotions of others. This more advanced step facilitates appropriate social development and socially appropriate interchange and activities.

Recognizing Emotions of Others
Once the child has made progress in recognizing and expressing his/her own emotions, the next steps involve learning to recognize the emotions of others and to understand as much as possible about the reasons and context in which they occur.

To assist the child in this endeavor, it is often helpful to engage in role play, acting out scenarios and events. For example, engage the child in a detailed examination of various scenarios to recognize emotional expressions and use this experience to put labels on the emotions revealed. In this way the child can begin to build up an internal representation of different scenarios en route to acquiring a better understanding of interpersonal situations and relationships.

Some critical skills include listening. Actively listening to understand what the other is trying to convey and learning to respond in a way that is complementary represent a substantive gain in interpersonal social skills. The first child may complain, for example, that he/she missed a favorite TV show; the second child could then empathize, noting that he/she has also had that experience. Sharing common experiences is a way to build friendships and shared interests.

The child with comorbid anxiety may need help to learn strategies to join other children in their play or activities. Acquiring some practiced routines that can be taken "off the shelf" so to speak and used as a guide in certain social situations can be instrumental in facilitating social bonds. Recognizing one's own emotions and the emotional tone of the particular group is an important skill for success.

The child with comorbid ADHD on the other hand will not only need to recognize his/her own emotional state and that of the others, but acquire some skills in self-control to find the right time to approach the group of children to seek entry. Approaching them while they are engaged in a tense exchange or at a critical point in a game they are playing will serve to alienate them from the child and lead to rejection. In this instance, the child must have sufficient self-control to correctly time the approach to the group based on his/her assessment of the group's activity, emotional tone, and readiness to receive a new entrant.

The ability to understand the perspective of the other is a critical skill in solving interpersonal problems. LI children may find this particularly challenging; it requires a sufficient understanding of one's own emotions, the relation between certain events and the range of emotions that another might have. In an attempt to extend an invitation to another child that would be appealing, some understanding of the things that child would enjoy will be important to consider when formulating the invitation. For instance, knowing that the other child likes to play video games but hates board games, the invitation could be framed to emphasize the former not the latter. Here some advance knowledge of the other child's preferences can be helpful. If this information is not available, the child can be prompted to simply ask the other child what things he/she likes to do or play.

Positive Reinforcement

The use of positive reinforcement can be a powerful tool in shaping behavior, but different approaches and the way in which they are implemented can have dramatically different consequences. The idea is to encourage the desired behavior and attitude by acknowledging that it represents a form of achievement or mastery. It is best to avoid presenting the issues as the parent versus the child, or the need for the child to be compliant; instead, the behavior and attitude should be identified as a step toward mastery, toward greater maturity, independence, and autonomy. Framing it in this way helps identify it as the child's individual goal and not one that can be perceived as a battle between the child and parents. Verbal praise should be supplemented with stickers, happy faces, and other forms of positive attention. Be sure that the LI child understands what is expected, and that he/she recognizes the behavior as a desirable goal. It may be necessary to go over the specifics with the child several times and to demonstrate what is expected to be certain they understand. Rewarding or praising behavior that approximates the target is often a sufficient first step. These rewards can be delivered over time and titrated till the target behavior is reliably achieved. The target behavior can be any behavior agreed upon between the child and parent and could refer to the child brushing his/her teeth without assistance, or discussing a scary topic such as worries about meeting new friends. When possible, coordination between home and school in providing the positive reinforcement is advisable, with particular attention to avoiding conflicting messages in which the child is praised at home, but similar behavior is ignored or discounted at school.

Clinical Pearl
Reinforce Child's Goals Toward Mastery and Maturity

In setting up reinforcement schedules, the tasks to be rewarded should be identified as the child's personal goals of steps toward mastery and maturity and not as something to please or satisfy the parent. If the latter, the behavior and the reward become the parents' issues, and the child can hold the parent ransom for ever-increasing rewards.

The potential downside to the use of positive reinforcement can occur in some instances in which parents will offer bribes as a reward for the behavior. This is more likely to occur if the situation has become one of parent versus child and the focus is on getting the child to comply. Unfortunately, this can easily become a situation in which the child escalates his or her demands, requiring greater and greater rewards to comply. Here the child will have gained control of the reinforcement schedule, and the parents will need to abandon that approach.

Limit Setting

In addition to praise and rewards, appropriate limits are essential. Limit setting provides the structure or boundaries within which the child behaves, but it also helps the child develop internal controls. Commonly, younger children and those with language delays are less able to simply internalize and transform verbal limits into behavior. Consequently, some form of physical limit, such as a time-out or being sent to their room, is a necessary step toward internalizing the limit.

Setting limits is essential to help the child develop internal controls

Example: One child, who had recently been introduced to time-outs for hitting his brother, soon began to play out this limit with his toys, giving them time-outs for misbehavior. The child is incorporating the limit so that it is now part of his own behavioral repertoire.

The parent must also be aware of the impact of the consequence or "punishment" on their child. This is especially important if the parent is upset and frustrated with their child. For instance, sometimes the offending behavior continues despite removing a privilege or invoking a punishment, and the parent may be tempted to escalate the punishment. Allan is punished for swearing, which provokes more swearing. The parent then ups the ante and threatens more severe punishment if the swearing continues. Allan not only continues swearing but increases the vulgarity level. In this circumstance, Allan may feel he no longer cares what the parent says or does, and continuing to raise the consequence drives the child even farther away, creating resentment and fracturing the previously established bond. Here it is best to state the consequence, indicate that you will discuss the issue further after tempers have cooled.

The parent or teacher will need to allow the LI children extra time to express their feelings and ideas

In setting a limit or implementing a consequence, counsel the parent to remind the child of the previously agreed upon plan concerning the particular behavior at issue. However, the LI child may be less capable of expressing fully his/her version of events or the rationale behind their behavior. The parent needs to be cognizant of these challenges and make accommodations by allowing the child more time to express himself or herself, by helping the child convey his or her ideas with prompts or even pictures if deemed appropriate. The parent should offer an opening empathic comment such as "you seemed pretty upset [or disappointed or have lots of mad feelings]." Sometimes simply repeating what the child has said or is doing will be perceived as empathic. For the LI child, repeating what he or she has said, or simply stating what the child is doing or the feeling he/she is conveying will be helpful in creating some dialogue or interchange. Wait for the child's response and in the continuing discussion, try to identify the feelings the child seems to be expressing and then label them – for instance: "It seems like you were scared [or afraid, or really mad, etc]." In this way you are giving the child tools with which to talk about his/her feelings instead of simply acting on them. The discussion may lead to a revision in the limit or consequence, or it may not, but in either situation, the child is more likely to feel heard or to perceive the decision as fair and acceptable than if the discussion had not occurred.

Strenghtening the Parent–Child Relationship

It is important to build opportunities for positive parent–child interactions. The situation and context in which this occurs is important. The parent should consider the amount of time the child will tolerate the particular activity before the child becomes disinhibited or on the verge of a meltdown. The situation or activity chosen should be one in which the parent has sufficient control so that the child is not relentlessly pestering the parent to buy him/her something. In other words, the activity chosen should be one with a minimal opportunity for conflict. The activity should be negotiated with the child, although the parent can offer the child a choice of two or three activities in keeping with the parent's goals of building a relationship with the child. In planning the outing and activity, preparing ahead of time is key to a successful outing. If on an outing, this means selecting appropriate snacks, drinks, simple games, or a small portable toy that can be taken along. Some contingency plan should be considered, in the event the outing goes poorly and an early retreat is needed. The experience serves as an example and lesson for future outings and the modifications needed to ensure success.

Children enjoy hearing stories their parents tell them. During one-on-one time with their child, parents can tell short stories of interest to the child. These can be a self-reference to the parent or parents; likewise, they can be imaginary stories built on themes that would interest the child and to which the child could relate, such as a story about a young boy or girl similar in age and who otherwise shares similar characteristics. These are opportunities to help the child acquire new words or phrases and to practice listening skills.

One-on-one time helps build relationships and can help build language skills

Promoting Proactive Parenting

Proactive parenting in which the parent plans and prepares to engage their child in child-focused activities can be instrumental in reducing conflict and improving behavior (Shelleby et al., 2012). In working with parents, scheduling enjoyable and goal-directed activities should be included as one of the therapeutic goals. To the extent that the activity chosen can be one that addresses more directly the child's particular difficulties, this would be preferable; however, caution the parent to be aware that in doing so, the child does not feel they are again "imposing therapy" on what is supposed to be fun. The point of this activity planning is to contribute to the child's general sense of well-being and positive mood, and to help build and/or repair key relationships.

Problem-Solving Skills

Once children acquire a problem-solving attitude, they will have taken an important developmental step and be on the road to developing these skills. The LI child may have greater challenges in acquiring these skills than the child with typically developing language. To be able to consider alternative strategies, to weigh the consequences, to consider the options, and to self-reward will ordinarily depend on a certain minimum language capability. Parents and other adults will need to help LI children acquire a problem-solving attitude and problem-solving skills. Ordinarily, the parent or other adult will need to work through and rehearse the issues and the potential solutions many times until the child gains some skill at problem solving.

In therapeutic settings, demonstrate and model a problem-solving attitude until children do it themselves

Developing a problem-solving attitude would be one of the targets in the therapy with the child. Here the therapist would review situations with the child to help him/her define the problems and identify a step-by-step approach to arrive at a series of alternative solutions. Over time with repeated practice, the child begins to internalize this approach and adopt it without prompting. In addition to the individual therapy, therapeutic groups consisting of a small group of children with varying degrees of skill at problem solving can be organized as part of the therapist's overall approach, or alternatively these groups can sometimes be organized through the child's school (Hemmeter, Ostrosky, & Fox, 2006). These groups are closely supervised and include some children who are able to problem solve and thereby serve as role models.

Anger Management

There are several important strategies to manage, modulate, and prevent anger displays. Identifying the triggers allows the child and adult to anticipate an outburst and to take steps to avoid the trigger. If that is neither possible nor desirable, the focus would turn to using words and language to express the anger or alternatively to defuse the intensity of the angry feelings.

LI children may be less able than typically developing children to identify the triggers and to bring them to the attention of the relevant adult. Often this requires complex language to explain that certain events are triggers, and the child may not have the requisite expressive language skills to do so. Additionally, discovering the triggers requires remembering and assembling several events or incidents in the proper sequence to arrive at the right conclusions. This would be challenging for most LI children. Consequently the child, parents, and other relevant adults need to assist in identifying the situations that may trigger outbursts. Adopting a daily diary in which the parent and child record events that may have triggered an outburst is often helpful in mapping the psychological landscape of the child's emotional reactions. Once this is established, it is then possible to go over these events with the child. With the younger and less competent child, it is advantageous to include the parents in this exercise.

Another strategy is to help the child learn the perspective of the other person with whom the child would be angry or in conflict. Teaching empathy and the other's point of view is intended to help neutralize or otherwise ameliorate the feelings of anger. Here again, working with the LI child may be more demanding and require additional strategies to help the child acquire the necessary empathic understanding. Learning to acquire the perspective of another person is imbedded in the therapeutic approach of learning to recognize one's own emotions and the emotions of other people. These skills though separable go hand in hand, and recognizing emotions in self and others is a prerequisite to recognizing the perspective of the other. (See "Recognizing Emotions of Others," for additional ideas on facilitating the development of empathy).

Still another strategy is to learn to anticipate the consequences of one's behavior. An adolescent boy with a history of explosive outbursts had learned to contain his behavior. He could anticipate the consequences of an outburst by reminding himself that "bad behavior" leads to bad consequences, but good behavior leads to good consequences. In this way, though he would still feel angry or upset, he was able to contain his behavioral reaction and address the issues in a more reasoned appropriate way.

Cognitive Self-Monitoring

> **Clinical Pearl**
> **Expressing Worries in the Metaphor of Play**
>
> Some children who are too anxious to discuss their feelings directly are able to use the metaphor of play to access and demonstrate their worries and fears. One 7-year-old girl enacted a scene in which she recruited a set of grandparents to move in with the parent figures so they could give the parents tips on how to be better parents. This girl could not and would not explicitly say that her parents needed help in parenting, but her play clearly conveyed her feeling that her parents needed help. This information provides material that can be explored with the parents.

Cognitive self-monitoring is an essential component in the cognitive therapy process. The child tracks his/her thoughts in the situations in which he/she has had difficulties. These may be situations in which they have been anxious, upset, or angry, or have been in conflict with their parents or teachers and peers, for example. The idea is to help the child see the connection between their feelings and thoughts and the specific event.

Children are taught to pay attention to their thoughts, to ask themselves questions such as, what am I thinking about, what am I feeling, what am I worried or upset about, what am I thinking might happen? Once the thoughts are recognized and the situation identified, the child can then begin to work on strategies to alter his or her thinking and feeling. It is critical that the child and, if necessary, the parents track the particular situations in which the child has been anxious, or had an angry or emotional outburst. The child must be able to recount or at least agree on what had transpired, and through this process learn that some feelings may be normal and that you can have a feeling without acting on it.

For instance, one girl became jealous and angry that her younger brother had been invited along to an event that she thought would be her exclusive privilege. Helping this girl to recognize that her feelings of jealousy and anger were normal and common was an important step forward for her. She was encouraged to speak to her parents about these feelings, and they could then reassure her (they had been primed to these issues in previous appointments) that separate arrangements would be made to address her need for some exclusive parental time.

Help the child to be as specific as possible about the situation and the feeling, and if possible, particularly with younger children, you will need to enlist the parents to help the child identify situations and feelings. It is through this process that errors in the child's thinking and conclusions are identified and negative thoughts are challenged and reframed.

For example, Colin, an 8-year-old boy, complained that his father hated him, and he in turn would say he wanted to kill his father. These thoughts and feelings would occur when his father would tell Colin that he had to stop playing his video game, or that he could not throw the ball against the kitchen wall, he had to go outside to play ball, for example. By reviewing these thoughts with Colin, Colin could see the connection between his father's action and his thought that his father hated him. Challenging Colin on this interpretation of his father's behavior, and getting Colin to check with his father led to a change in his thinking and a reduction in the intensity of his anger with his father.

Make use of cartoons and thought bubbles to help the child express and convey his/her thoughts and feelings. With the LI child these scenarios may need to be acted out with puppets or toy animals. Using these concrete materials helps children express their feelings, worries, and anger and brings those into the therapeutic realm. The use of play materials also puts some distance between the child and the feelings, and consequently, for children too anxious to discuss their feelings directly, they become more accessible in the metaphor of the play. This process can also be usefully employed to challenge errors in thinking and to reinforce positive thoughts.

Desensitization and Exposure

Work with the child to catalogue the list of situations in which he/she is worried, or becomes angry and upset. Help the child to rate the intensity of the feeling and how common or frequent it is. This can be done with a fever thermometer, ladder, or similar device, for instance, in which the strongest feelings are at the top of the thermometer, and below which are ranked the other worries or problem feelings needing attention. Identify a situation or problem with which to start. This will be a gradual process in which children will begin at the lowest level on the thermometer with which they are comfortable and gradually work their way up the scale, until they are able to confront the situation without becoming anxious or upset.

Help the child develop a catalogue of fears and worries that will become the therapeutic target

For the LI child with comorbid anxiety, the child should identify as many situations as he/she can in which he/she gets frightened or scared. You can assist by asking questions about situations you are aware of from discussions with the parents. Once the list of fearful situations is generated, help him/her place them in a hierarchy from the most intense or severe to the least. Some children enjoy using a fever thermometer to scale their fears. This may take several sessions and can be revised as the sessions progress. Once this catalogue of fears and worries is created, the next task is to select the situation or event with which to start. This will lead to a process of desensitization, starting with situations real or imagined with tolerable anxiety, and working your way up the thermometer to eventually face and overcome the anxiety at the top of the thermometer.

Desensitization and exposure are usually paired. Children will gradually work their way up the hierarchy of feared situations or experiences, starting with the situation that evokes the least anxiety, and once they are no longer anxious facing or thinking about that specific situation, they can then move on to the next feared situation in the hierarchy. Eventually, the child will confront the actual feared object or situation at the top of the thermometer and by repeated exposure will come to master the situation and no longer experience the anxiety.

Acquiring Positive Self-Talk

Self-talk is an essential skill in learning to manage intense emotions

Self-talk and other cognitive restructuring interventions help develop coping skills (Kendall & Suveg, 2006). Self-talk is an essential skill in learning to manage anger and other intense emotions. Learning alternative explanations to interpretations of hostile intent is facilitated by self-talk; self-talk also leads to self-instruction, learning to "defang" the offending individual or traumatic event.

Using the child's own language and terminology, the therapist rehearses with the child or youth the consequences of the angry outbursts, and helps them to acknowledge the unfavorable outcomes. As children progress in their ability to talk to themselves, to anticipate future events, they also learn the consequences of angry outbursts. Through practiced self-talk, the child acquires the ability to remind himself/herself when in the real-life situation of the consequences of acting on his/her anger. This then results in learning to express that anger in more socially appropriate ways. Other self-talk strategies to help control angry and upset feelings include learning to devalue certain comments, to trivialize them, to make a joke of them, or to ignore them ('who cares what they say"). These are all strategies to help take the sting out of an unkind comment or experience that may leave the child feeling angry and upset. Through this process of self-talk, children learn to gain greater control of their behavior.

Clinical Pearl
Feelings are Neither Right nor Wrong

Feelings are neither right nor wrong, but convey information. Help the child attend to their feelings and emotions in the varied and diverse situations of everyday life. This can help them learn about themselves and the people with whom they interact. Once the feeling is recognized, they need to understand what provoked that feeling and what if anything they should do. Careful analysis of the situation that provoked the feeling should inform the behavior. A goal in therapy is to help the child acquire the skills to do this without the therapist's support and guidance.

Identify as well negative self-talk, i.e., talk that is demeaning or blaming or conveys a sense of helplessness. Help the child challenge this negative self-talk and acquire a more forgiving, tolerant, and positive self-attitude. This does not mean the child is free of responsibility for his/her behavior. The child must learn to accept responsibility for his/her behavior. Children and adolescents need to learn that while we cannot control how we feel, we can control what we do about the feelings we have and how we behave. We can learn to manage our feelings and our behavior. Talking to ourselves, to educate and train ourselves is basic strategy to deal with strong emotions, such as anger.

Compared with the typically developing child, the LI child will have more difficulty acquiring the ability to use self-talk. Here the therapist can be helpful in supplying phrases that the child can rehearse and practice. These will need to be adapted to the child's language level of competency and will likely require the use of shorter, simpler statements that the child can repeat. The therapist will need to review this to be sure the child has internalized their meanings and can remember to use these phrases appropriately.

Supplying words and phrases for the LI child to practice and rehearse will help them develop skills in self-talk

Sometimes the best strategy is to wait and allow time to pass and the intensity of the angry feelings to dissipate. In the interim the child can engage in self-talk, to talk himself or herself down – for example, that it was not intentional, that it is not that important – and to remind oneself to stop and plan what to do in what would be a socially appropriate response.

Anticipating Consequences/Outcomes

Children with LI, especially those with language comprehension difficulties, (Beitchman, 1985) compared with typically developing children have greater difficulties with being flexible and shifting from one situation to another; they are more likely to be rigid in their thinking and to depend on the predictability and sameness of their environment to maintain an even psychological state. Consequently, with change, especially unexpected change (surprise and disappointment), children and more commonly LI children will become upset. Because children have little control over their environment and are dependent on their parents and other adults, when change is unexpected, and when promises are broken or when planned events do not materialize as anticipated, especially if the event is highly valued, the child is likely to be upset with varying degrees of intensity, from mild displays of temper to a full-blown meltdown.

LI children will have difficulty with change and transitions; they will need guidance and practice with transitions

It is important to help children anticipate that not all things can be guaranteed, that sometimes for reasons beyond our control, events do not unfold as planned. The child will need help to anticipate these possibilities. The younger child and the child with LI will need some rehearsal in the potential disappointment and contingency plans to deal with the disappointment.

It is useful to help prepare the child for the inevitable disappointment and to develop strategies to manage the feelings and the event. When the child has made progress at acquiring a new skill or in mastering a behavioral or developmental challenge, the child and parent should be prepared for possible setbacks, recognizing that the setbacks are not permanent but instead representative of the zigzag path that is common in progressing to greater maturity.

Relaxation Techniques

Progressive muscle relaxation is a traditional relaxation strategy used to treat a variety of symptoms (Weisz & Bearman, 2008). This technique involves progressively tensing and relaxing individual muscles until the body is relaxed. With children, it is best to focus on large muscle groups, such as arms, stomach, legs, and the whole body, such that the progression does not take too long and to ensure that the children are able to control these muscle groups. The child should progress from one body region to another until most of the major muscle groups are relaxed. Training can begin in the therapeutic office, and children should be encouraged to practice relaxation once or twice a day.

Deep breathing exercises are a regular, common component in relaxation training. They are helpful in counterbalancing hyperventilation and reducing tension and decreasing the sensations associated with anxiety. These exercises are often paired with progressive muscle relaxation to assist in lowering the level of anxiety

Advocacy

There is strong evidence that the LI child and youth is at increased risk for a variety of adverse outcomes. LI girls are at increased risk of being sexually abused (Brownlie, Jabbar, Beitchman, Vida, & Atkinson, 2007), and LI males are at increased risk of being arrested and incarcerated (Zenz & Langelett, 2004). Because LI is often an invisible handicap, this concomitant increased vulnerability is often not recognized.

Acting as an advocate for the child or youth is an important component in the overall treatment approach. The clinician/therapist should advocate on behalf of these youngsters. Parents, teachers, and other responsible adults need to be made aware of their increased vulnerability, and steps should be taken to ensure increased safety. For youths who have been arrested or incarcerated, they will need assistance to properly instruct their counsel. Given their LI, these youths may fail to properly instruct counsel or to fully understand the judicial process and consequently may end up wrongly convicted or sentenced more severely than would be justified had they been able to fully and properly defend themselves (Lavigne & Van Rybroek, 2010; Snow & Powell, 2012).

4.1.6 Therapeutic Considerations for Adolescents With LI

Psychotherapy can be usefully employed with LI youths struggling with issues related to self-esteem, identity formation, role definition, and interpersonal problems, among others. Established models of therapy that would traditionally be used for specific clinical conditions or developmental struggles can be modified to take differences in the language abilities of the individual into account. Rigid adherence to established, traditional models of therapy may serve to exclude people with LIs who might nevertheless benefit from therapy.

Psychotherapy creates an opportunity for participants to express themselves in a supportive environment and which allows them to feel included and valued. Individuals with LI and learning disabilities are vulnerable to psychiatric disturbances and to common developmental challenges in establishing an identity; they may struggle with problems of separation and differentiation from parents. Given their LIs, these issues are likely to be more challenging and more common than with youths with typically developing language. This is because they may be less able to express and defend the need for age-appropriate changes in the parent child relationship.

This youth needed a very deliberate and sensitive approach when communicating with him. It was evident that when communication was ambiguous, he was prone to become suspicious that he would be exploited or

Case Vignette 6
Language Disorder and Comorbid Conduct Disorder

Tom was seen in a court-ordered psychiatric assessment. He presented as a tall, handsome youngster, who looked older than his stated age of 17. He had an athletic muscular build and conveyed an intimidating presence.

Tom reported that his first robbery was committed a year earlier when he was caught by the security guard at a liquor store with a bottle of hard liquor in his pocket. Approximately one month later, he was caught with a stolen Dodge Caravan by police in four police cars. He was also charged with possession of a concealed weapon. Tom has difficulty controlling his anger. When angry he has punched holes in his wall and closet, thrown things in his room, and slammed the door.

He says his triggers occur when he does not understand the situation, when he is confused, when he is not treated fairly, and when he is being lied to. For example, he feels betrayed by his legal aid lawyer because he says he did not know about this particular psychiatric assessment. He feels that "everyone is against" him and "everyone gangs up on" him.

Tom worries that the judge does not know him well enough to decide on his sentencing. He believes that the judge will view him as "just another violent guy with guns who hits people, having sex with girls constantly, attempting murder and assaulting others, times five." He describes himself as funny, athletic, understanding, and easy to talk to. He would like the judge to know that he has "done stupid stuff" and that he is "willing to change," but he "can't do it in custody."

During the interview, Tom had difficulty understanding questions being asked. They had to be repeated, restated, rephrased, and reworded. Tom gets irritable and appears intimidating at these times.

Tom's verbal comprehension ability was found to be in the 3rd percentile; Tom's perceptual reasoning ability (i.e., problem solving with visually presented materials) fell within the average range, in the 39th percentile. His overall reading skills fell in the 2nd percentile and were comparable to those of a student in elementary school Grades 4–6. Tom did not fall within the mental retardation classification, yet he had severe and serious cognitive deficits, primarily in the language domain.

otherwise disadvantaged. The issue was further compounded because of his impulsive style of responding and his difficulties with verbal comprehension. Adults, teachers, and youths with whom he was likely to interact would assume that he understood what was said as well as any other youth his age. Inevitably, situations would arise in which he would not understand what was being said; though the communication was entirely innocent, he would assume some sinister intent and might react impulsively and aggressively. As with the children in Case Vignettes 2 and 3, verbal communication should be aimed at his level of comprehension, using short, clear sentences, appropriately paced to be certain that Tom has understood what is being said. It is important that Tom recognize that he has challenges in verbal comprehension, and that adults speaking to and with him avoid any suggestion of being condescending or talking down to him.

In addition to working with key members of the youth's environment, such as his teachers, parents, coaches, and others, he is an excellent candidate for specific therapy targeting his internal scripts and the need for cognitive restructuring. Self-talk interventions are essential in anger control training.

Individual Therapeutic Approaches

The first step will be to establish a working alliance with this youth. This can be facilitated by conveying warmth and friendliness and actively working to form a positive relationship with Tom. LI individuals may benefit from slightly looser therapeutic boundaries, and using a friendlier less rigid manner which may include occasionally extending the therapeutic session. The therapist will need to be more active than would be the case with a youth with typical language development.

As with younger children, establishing a therapeutic contract in which the youth is able to articulate his goals is a key ingredient to success. Identifying one's goals in therapy is not quite as straightforward as it may seem. The focus needs to be on achievable and realistic goals that are within the capability of the youth. Consequently, it may take several sessions to help the youth clarify and discover his particular therapeutic goals. A variety of therapeutic models are thought to be helpful; flexibility in working with the LI youth to achieve the therapeutic goals is paramount. Using adaptive forms of mainstream CBT approaches, including nonverbal materials, visual aids, and simple cues, changes can be demonstrated and can be useful adjuncts to the ongoing therapy, used as a means to help the youth express himself and to facilitate engagement with the therapist. Adaptations include the use of drawing, photographs, role play, stories, drama, art, and other narrative approaches. In addition, there are picture books for adults that can be used with LI youths as an aid in the therapeutic process. Topics may include bereavement, abuse, making relationships, depressed mood, being at home, and being in therapy.

As already noted, LI youths may have difficulties perceiving and correctly identifying emotional states in themselves and others, and CBT approaches can help these youths to acquire skills aimed at self-control of anger and emotional self-regulation. These CBT approaches include self-talk interventions focused on self-instruction, reattribution, and alternatives to hostile explanations.

Because of the potential difficulty, the adolescent with LI may encounter in generalizing from the therapeutic situation to experiences of everyday life, practice and support between sessions and after therapy is finished may be necessary. The effectiveness of the therapy can be enhanced with a supportive and resourceful network for the youth.

LI youths will feel challenged in trying to express the full range of emotions and may seem passive in the therapeutic encounter. Similar to others, they will have difficulty expressing negative feelings toward people on whom they depend. Drawing out the youth to verbalize these feelings in the safety of the therapeutic office can be a key therapeutic process. Discussions need to be managed carefully to avoid generating debilitating guilt and to help guide the youth regarding the appropriate time and place to express these feelings outside the safety of the therapeutic office. One useful strategy is to organize a family session with the youth and his/her parents to help them discuss some of the youth's concerns. Because of the youth's LI, he/she may need the therapist's support to fully convey his/her thoughts feelings and concerns to the parents in a way that they are able to respond to constructively. Typically, this may take several sessions spread over weeks and sometimes months to achieve satisfactory progress. See the next section "The Family" for further discussion of these points.

> **Helping youths identify intense emotions toward significant others needs to be carefully managed to avoid generating debilitating guilt**

The Family

The relationship between the youth and his/her family is often a central issue in therapy. The youth may experience his/her family as supportive, and the family may be mobilized to assist in ways that promote growth, individuation, autonomy, and developmentally appropriate independence.

> **When the youth and family are in conflict, managing the conflict becomes pivotal to successful therapy**

When the youth and family are in conflict, managing the conflict becomes pivotal to successful therapy. Parents are often legitimately concerned to understand how their adolescent is progressing in therapy. You will need to support the parents while maintaining the youth's confidentiality; this is a common therapeutic challenge. This can be even more challenging with LI adolescents who are unable to effectively convey to their parents their need to have their therapy be confidential, or to express their point of view clearly on a range of subjects.

Support can be delivered by conveying empathy to the parents about their concerns and offering advice and encouragement on tactics and activities they can pursue to assist their son or daughter. With the consent and knowledge of the youth, you can offer some general comments on their progress in therapy. Depending on the nature of the issues, you may schedule joint sessions with the youth and the parents. In doing so, be sure to articulate a clear agenda of the goals of the session – for example, to have the parents listen to their son's or daughter's explicit concerns. For the LI youths, you will need to rehearse what they propose to tell their parents, and during the session, you will need to be vigilant that the parents are listening to their child. You may need to repeat, rephrase, and elaborate on what the youth is saying or trying to say, while maintaining a respectful and empathic attitude to the parents and the youth.

Depending on the nature of the parental issues, it may be best to refer the parents to a colleague who can independently offer them therapeutic support. The work with the parents will be directed to the specific issues uncovered over the course of the assessment. It can be focused on helping the parents deal with the issues concerning their youth, for instance, or directed at marital, parenting, or mental health issues that they themselves identify.

4.1.7   Social Skills Training Programs

There are several social skills training (SST) programs that can be usefully employed to supplement individual therapies. A brief description of some common elements and approaches of the more enduring programs are outlined below.

To develop and improve socially appropriate behavior for children with LI, SST programs use a combination of different cognitive and behavioral intervention models such as (a) direct instruction, (b) modeling, (c) shaping, (d) rehearsal, and (e) feedback (Jones, Sheridan, & Binns, 1993; Kavale & Mostert, 2004). The interventions for various social skills also focus on improving behaviors including anger control, asking for help, responding to aggression, negotiation, asking for information, working collaboratively, and demonstrating appropriate emotions and expression of feelings (Goldstein, Click, & Gibbs, 1998; Patterson et al., 1989).

Direct instruction will need to be tailored to the child's ability to understand and remember instructions. These instructions usually include defining the skill, describing reasons to practice the skill, examples where the skill will be useful, the steps necessary to carry out the skill, and some rules about when the skill is to be used (Elliott & Busse, 1991; Walker, Colvin, & Ramsey, 1995). Direct instruction with the LI child sets the stage for the expectations, but by itself it will not be sufficient.

Use modeling techniques to demonstrate the social skill through live performance, videotapes, audiotapes, or pictorial models (Walker et al., 1995). This procedure provides the child with a sequential representation of the behavioral components involved. Seeing it demonstrated is a powerful way for the child to learn the specific behavior.

You can shape behavior by reinforcing the appropriate skill or behavior or something close to it. In this approach, you will need to wait until the child shows behaviors that are not ordinarily shown but are similar enough to the desired behavior to be reinforced.

Rehearsal and feedback procedures are typically performed together. Verbal rehearsal is most common, in which children verbally rehearse the steps in sequence to perform the skill. Rehearsal can also include structured practices such as role playing, so the child can put his or her skills into action. Following the rehearsal, the child receives feedback on his or her performance from other children and from the instructor. Positive reinforcement will encourage the child to practice the social skill outside of the treatment settings (Spence, 2003).

Two SST programs that incorporate a combination of different procedures to teach social skills, one for school-age children and the other for toddlers, are briefly described below.

School-Age Children

Skillstreaming (Goldstein, Spranfkin, Gershaw, & Klein, 1979) has become one of the most widely used SST approaches over 2 decades among children and adolescents. Skillstreaming targets both verbal and nonverbal social cues. This intervention was partly derived from Albert Bandura's social learning theory (1973) and encompasses strategies of modeling, behavioral rehearsal, and social reinforcement. The constituent procedures for skillstreaming are defining the social skill, modeling the skill, conducting role play, providing performance feedback, and generalization training.

The Toddler or Young Child

Because social functioning involves different skills at each developmental period, SST programs that effectively improve the social skills among school-aged children may not apply to preschool children (Choi & Kim, 2003; Guralnick & Neville, 1997). Interventions aimed at introducing prosocial behaviors to toddlers focus on interactions between the child and the parent/caregiver, the type of play activity, and the quality of peer relationships. The most commonly employed techniques to improve social skills include (1) prompting and rehearsal of target behaviors, (2) play-related activities, (3) free-play generalization, (4) reinforcement of appropriate behaviors, (5) modeling of specific social skills, and (6) direct instruction of social skills (Vaughn et al., 2003).

Adjusting Language to the Level of the Child

When designing paradigms and strategizing treatment plans to improve social communication for children with comorbid LI, clinicians must keep in mind the existing language barriers that may influence the learning outcomes (Brinton & Fujiki, 2006). Many SST programs have language as the primary vehicle of instruction. Moreover, language plays a pivotal role in facilitating communication between the child and his or her peers. Often, the language demands may be taxing for children with LI to the degree that they are left with low cognitive resources for social reflection. Consequently, SST programs should adjust the language levels to that of the child. The use of visual, tactile, and contextual cues may also be incorporated in SST programs to enhance the learning experience for children with LI (Delonia & Pettigrew, 1998).

A plethora of SST programs have been developed over the past 30 years to help promote positive social relationships among children with social deficits. Although SST programs have become a popular treatment, they should be viewed as an experimental intervention (Kavale & Mostert, 2004). The research and educational community have not been able to arrive at the most ideal SST program, largely due to the lack of consensus among researchers and practitioners regarding implementation procedures, and which social skills to target (Jones, Sheridan, & Binns, 1993). For the most part, SST has been shown to be effective in improving the social behaviors of students with emotional and behavior in a limited number of settings for certain periods of time on a wide range of measured outcomes, which include academic success in school as well as positive relationships with family, peers, and adults (Chen, 2006).

> The use of visual, tactile, and contextual cues can be usefully employed to enhance the learning experience for LI children

Therapeutic Games

There are a variety of board games that are excellent adjuncts to the therapeutic process (Streng, 2008). Some of these games build on the cognitive therapy model in drawing connections between thoughts, feelings, behavior, and problem solving. They can be presented as a fun activity, are nonthreatening, and typically will engage the child emotionally. Some of these games come with helpful DVDs. Games offer an in vivo example of some of the issues with which the child may be struggling, and the game provides an opportunity to practice strategies that will help the child with a particular problem. The LI child may especially benefit from the use of these games since they do not depend on traditional talk therapies, and the LI child will experience them as less taxing. See Table 11 for a list of some popular board games.

Table 11

Therapeutic Games

Game	Age	Description
Anger Control Game (Berg, 1990a)	8–13	Teaches child the skills they need to control anger. Game is particularly helpful in treating children with conduct disorders or those with temper control problems.
Self-Control Game (Berg, 1990b)	8–13	Teaches children how to exercise self-control in academic and social settings, and addresses traits and behaviors that are classified as impulsive, inattentive, or hyperactive. Teaches children how to change maladaptive behavior.
Helping, Sharing, and Caring Game (Gardner, 1998)	4–11	Game focuses on developing children's concepts of sympathy, empathy, ethics, values, personal relationships, self-esteem, health, and consideration for others.
Best Behavior Game (Shapiro, 2007)	6–12	Helps children distinguish between appropriate and inappropriate behavior, recognize personal boundaries, communicate effectively, and develop problem-solving skills. Game helps oppositional and noncompliant children move toward positive behavior.
Talking, Feeling and Doing Game (Gardner, 1973)	5–16	Engages the resistant child in meaningful psychotherapeutic endeavors, focusing on specific problems or concerns.
Drugs and Alcohol Game (Berg, 1989)	10–18	Game presents specific scenarios in which characters confront alcohol, cocaine, marijuana, and pills using skills to resist the internal and external pressures to experiment with the substances.
Let's Get Rational (Wilde, 1990)	11–18	Helps children recognize and change irrational thinking that may cause emotional distress, and gives them an opportunity to acknowledge the power of their thoughts on emotions.

4.2   Mechanisms of Action

Here are some central tenets to guide the therapeutic intervention with children with language delays and comorbid conditions:

4.2.1   Working With the Environment

First, ensure that the environment is as ecologically accommodating as possible, but not so accommodating that the child has little incentive to progress toward less accommodation. Fewer distractions and less noise lower the cognitive demands on the child; this together with an extra level of support reduces the child's stress level and anxious worry. Experiencing less stress, allows more cognitive resources to be directed to learning the material presented and a focus on gaining skills in the areas of his/her deficit (Kahneman, 2011). Working with the child's family and school to reduce known stressors, and to identify strategies that can preempt behavioral outbursts or anxious meltdowns will help lower the tension and anxiety the child experiences and help interrupt the cycle of conflict and punishment that can be so debilitating and discouraging for both the child and his/her family.

4.2.2   Working With the Child

Intervention for Speech and Language
(1) Working with the child: Specific training and practice in the areas of deficit contribute to improved performance in several different domains. For instance, focused training in single-word decoding and phonological processing leads to gains in reading. It is hypothesized that phonological processing skills are a prerequisite to word decoding, and improvements in one area are evident in the other.
(2) Speech and language therapy helps build vocabulary, improves understanding of grammatical structures, and helps children progress in recognizing the sequence of events to understand causality – for example, in the sentence "the boy tipped the glass then the milk spilled on the floor and the cat licked it up." Learning to understand and express causal sequences has several important benefits: It will make it easier for the child to understand and respond to his/her teacher, it should lead to improved grades, and it allows the child to participate in ordinary discourse with friends without feeling out of place or stupid or being teased. There should be evidence of a reduction in the level of the child's behavioral and emotional problems.

Behavioral and Emotional Problems
The children who respond to treatment will have gained skills and abilities to self-regulate their emotions, to anticipate events, and recognize the consequence of his/her actions. The child will have learned methods to "cool down" instead of reacting angrily and impulsively. Through the process of therapy the child will have acquired the skills and techniques to control his/her

behavior and to regulate his/her emotions. Some of these gains are dependent on learning techniques of self-talk, of facing and overcoming certain feared events or situations, and developing a better understanding of other people's emotions. Learning to recognize emotions in self and others assists in social interactions.

4.3   Efficacy and Prognosis

Reliable information on the efficacy of intervention for language disorders comorbid with an Axis 1 diagnosis is scant. However, there is information on on the efficacy of interventions for anxiety disorders and for the DBDs including ADHD. The extent to which treatment effects will be similar among those without and with a comorbid language disorder remains an empirical question still to be answered.

4.3.1   Anxiety Disorders

The most commonly practiced treatment plans for anxiety disorders among children and adolescents encompass cognitive behavioral approaches, which include exposure techniques, cognitive restructuring strategies, relaxation techniques, and positive self-talk. Family-focused treatment programs also teach parents how to cope with child anxiety, ways to effectively communicate with the child, as well as strategies to manage the parents' own anxiety. The overall mean effect size of treatment was reported to be 0.86, with individual-based, group-focused, and family-focused intervention programs equally efficacious in treating childhood anxiety. Reported treatment effects were maintained up to several years posttreatment, ranging from moderate effects ($d_{es} = 0.61$) to very large effects ($d_{es} = 1.13$) over follow-up assessments conducted between 10.4 months and 7.4 years after treatment (In-Albon & Schneider, 2007).

4.3.2   Disruptive Behavior Disorders: ADHD / ODD / CD

Emerging evidence suggests that a multimodal approach to ADHD that includes pharmacological treatment along with behavioral parent training (BPT), behavioral school intervention, and skills training seems to better address the multifaceted needs of children (Watson, Richels, Michalek, & Raymer, 2012).

Overall, BPT and cognitive behavioral interventions produce the most favorable treatment outcomes in the child's behavior (Linseisen, 2006). Nevertheless, the treatment effect sizes for children with ODD and CD are modest in magnitude, and are unlikely to produce long-lasting changes in the child's behavior. Programs that combine affective, social, behavioral, and cognitive components across different settings (i.e., home, school, and clinic) would be most beneficial in prolonging treatment gains that would also allow for generalization to community settings. Despite the popularity and recognized positive effects of BPT, the available evidence is not strong enough to form a basis for unequivocal clinical practice guidelines (Zwi, Jones, Thorgaard, York, & Dennis, 2011).

SST when paired with behavioral interventions that invite parents and/or teachers to reinforce skills taught in sessions with the child when he/she is at home or when interacting in a more natural environment appears to be more beneficial than stand-alone SST intervention. Indeed there is evidence that behavioral and cognitive behavioral group-based parenting interventions are effective and cost-effective for improving child conduct problems, parental mental health, and parenting skills in the short term (Furlong et al., 2012*).

4.4   Variations and Combinations of Methods

4.4.1   Use of Medication

There are no indications for the use medication to treat the language delays in the LI child. However, among LI children with a comorbid condition such as ADHD/ADD or anxiety, the same indications that apply to the comorbid Axis 1 condition would apply to the child with the comorbid disorder. Treat the comorbid Axis 1 condition with the same medication you would if the child did not have a comorbid language delay. Short-term reports of academic gains among children with reading disabilities and ADD are known. Long-term medication use is also associated with improvements in standardized achievement scores. However, the magnitude of these improvements is small, and their clinical or educational significance is questionable. Evidence for long-term improvements in school grades and grade retention is less compelling (Langberg & Becker, 2012). The mechanism of action is understood to be due to the enhanced ability to concentrate (Table 12).

Children with a diagnosis of ADHD/ADD or a DBD with ADHD are known to respond to psychostimulant medication. Medications based on methylphenidate hydrochloride and dextroamphetamine sulphate have a long history of use and have been shown to result in behavior change in the short term, providing evidence of their short-term efficacy. In recent years, long-acting formulations have been developed and have achieved widespread acceptance; an important advantage of these medications is that they only require single daily dosing, in contrast to earlier preparations that were short acting and needed to be taken two or more times a day.

Many families initially resist the idea of medication for their child. Do not try to convince them that they should try the medication but simply inform them of the risks and benefits and be open to further discussion about the use of medication. The medication is not intended to cure the child's problems but can be of assistance in helping the child gain control of his/her behavior and can serve as an important bridge upon which to build or repair friendships, relationships with parents and teachers, and contribute to improvements in his/her self-esteem. The medication is not a panacea, but does offer certain advantages. It may also help make the child more accessible to learning and to academic gains.

Psychostimulant
medication has been
shown to be effective
in short-term
treatment of ADHD.
Long-term efficacy is
less compelling

For the child with a comorbid language delay and ADHD/ADD, the medication should never be considered as a sufficient by itself, but as part of a comprehensive treatment approach in which other psychosocial interventions, as discussed above, are included as well.

Children or adolescents with a diagnosis of comorbid language delay and anxiety disorder would be considered candidates for medication if they do not respond to psychotherapeutic attempts and symptoms continue or worsen.

Table 12
Medications for Use With ADHD and Anxiety Disorders Comorbid With LI

ADHD/ADD and comorbid language impairment

Class of medications	**Psychostimulants** The psychostimulants commonly used to treat the symptoms of ADHD include: 1. Methylphenidate (Ritalin): There is an immediate-acting and a slow-release version. 2. Concerta: This is a long-acting form of methylphenidate that is slowly absorbed into the bloodstream and has 12-hour duration. 3. Dexedrine Spansule: This is an immediate-acting form of amphetamine. 4. Adderall XR is a long-acting version of Dexedrine. Has both immediate release and long-acting effects. 5. Vyvanse: The generic name is lisdexamfetamine dimesylate. This is an inactive prodrug which is converted to the pharmacologically active dextroamphetamine in the blood stream. **Atomoxetine** (Strattera) This is a norepinephrine reuptake inhibitor and is considered to be in different class from the psychostimulants. It is commonly used when a psychostimulant has been discontinued because of adverse effects.
Indications	These medications are indicated for the treatment of symptoms of ADHD. This includes the core symptoms of distractibility, difficulties sustaining attention, impulsivity, and certain behavioral problems such as oppositional behavior.
Adverse effects	1. Initial insomnia 2. Decreased appetite and weight loss 3. Abdominal pain 4. Headache 5. Palpitations 6. Increase in heart rate and blood pressure 7. Dysphoria, irritability 8. Potential increase in tics 9. Some reduction in ultimate growth height
Contraindications	Allergic, history of cardiac problems, hyperthyroidism, and psychosis.

Table 12 (continued)

Anxiety disorders with comorbid language delays

Class of medication	**Selective Serotonin Reuptake Inhibitors (SSRIs)**
	The medications used to treat children and adolescents with anxiety disorders are SSRIs, which are considered antidepressants even though they are efficacious in the treatment of anxiety disorders.
	Fluoxetine (Prozac) and sertraline (Zoloft) are the two medications most commonly prescribed for the treatment of anxiety disorders in children and adolescents. These two drugs have US Food and Drug Administration approval for the treatment of non-OCD anxiety disorders in children and adolescents.
Indications	The indications for the use of SSRIs are the presence of anxiety disorder, or significant anxiety symptoms that interfere with functioning. Anxiety symptoms would manifest as a social phobia, for example, or generalized anxiety disorder, in which the child expresses intense worries about common, everyday events and occurrences
Adverse effects	Adverse effects of SSRIs: 1. Gastrointestinal symptoms (decreased appetite, dry mouth, nausea, vomiting) 2. Dizziness 3. Insomnia, sedation 4. Activation (e.g., symptoms of hyperactivity, agitation, or silliness) 5. Akathisia (restlessness) 6. Irritability, sweating 7. Changes in appetite 8. Symptoms of sexual dysfunction 9. Potential increased suicidal thinking. Studies have shown a very low risk and no studies report increased rates of actual suicides.
Contraindications	Hypersensitivity, current use of monoamine oxidase inhibitor
	Given the concern regarding the increased rate of suicidal ideation among individuals taking SSRIs, children started on SSRIs should be monitored closely.

Note. ADD = attention deficit disorder; ADHD = attention-deficit/hyperactivity disorder; LI = language impairment; OCD = obsessive compulsive disorder.

Antidepressant medication has been used successfully with anxious children (Walkup et al., 2008). The most commonly prescribed medications for anxiety disorders in children and adolescents are known as selective serotonin reuptake inhibitors (SSRIs). Although considered antidepressants they have been shown to be efficacious in the treatment of anxiety disorders. These medications reduce anxiety and allow the child to participate more fully in age-appropriate activities at school and in the neighborhood with classmates and

Selective serotonin reuptake inhibitors have been used successfully to treat anxiety disorders in children

peers. In this way the child gradually gains confidence to speak and participate with other children, both learning how to do so and gaining confidence through this process. Studies show that the best results are obtained by the combination of SSRIs and CBT (Walkup et al., 2008). Depending on the acuity and severity of the anxiety disorder, psychotherapy would be tried initially, and medication added if the response was judged to be inadequate.

4.5   Problems in Carrying Out the Treatments

4.5.1   Working With Parents

Because progress is often slow, the parents and or child may resist continuing in therapy and cut short the treatment before the full impact can take effect. Parents should be told at the outset what to expect in terms of the child's progress and the duration of therapy, and cautioned on the concern regarding early dropout.

Keeping the parent well informed on the child's progress in therapy will help the parent feel engaged in the process and more inclined to support the ongoing work.

In those situations in which the parents are enlisted as cotherapists for their child – for example, in the Hanen Early Language Parent Program (Manolson, 1979) – it is critically important for the therapist to be accessible and supportive to the parents. Regular face-to-face meetings to review tape-recorded sessions of the specific techniques are an invaluable component to the ongoing stability of the program. There are other therapist–parent models in which the speech/language pathologist assists parents in learning and utilizing language facilitation and responsively training techniques. Responsivity training is based on the assumption that parents' responses to young children's communication strongly influence the child's early language development (Kamhi et al., 2007; Wood, 2007). These techniques have been found to accelerate growth in overall word use (Fey et al., 2006).

4.5.2   Addressing Pragmatic Issues

A range of other pragmatic issues inevitably arise, such as problems with transportation, canceled appointments and family crises that interfere with the ongoing appointments. Therapist absences due to illness, vacations, and schedule conflicts all can fracture the momentum of the therapy and pose the danger of premature termination.

To the extent that make-up appointments are possible to maintain the momentum of the therapy, this is to be encouraged. Advising the family and child ahead of time of any known interruptions in the therapist's schedule can mitigate some of the untoward impact of the absences.

Therapy should occur in the same room each time and any toys, games, books, or other materials used in the therapy should be available throughout the therapy. Deviations or changes in the room or the available materials can disrupt the therapeutic process, but unless these are repeated occurrences, they should not normally lead to premature termination of the therapy. To the extent that the therapist is aware of these potential disruptions, the child/youth should be alerted to them ahead of time.

4.5.3   Therapist–Client Relationship

The child or youth should help identify and agree with the goals of therapy and be motivated to participate in the therapy and the therapeutic process. Problems are likely to arise when the child/youth feels that therapy has been imposed and he/she does not share the goals of therapy, or denies that therapy is needed or desirable. These issues must be negotiated prior to beginning therapy, and their successful resolution is a precondition to beginning treatment.

In some instances the initial goals of engagement may be to educate the youth about the therapeutic process, and to motivate him/her to participate in therapy. Through a process of motivational interviewing, the youth is helped to identify personal goals which through the process of therapy may become more readily attainable, and the youth then becomes more inclined to pursue therapy to attain those goals.

Equally important, the child must feel positively toward the therapist and the therapy; otherwise, the parent may have difficulty getting the child to the therapy, and the child may be too resistant to benefit. Intermixing play and engaging the child in activities that he/she likes and enjoys while incorporating enriched language stimulation offers one approach to maintaining the child in the ongoing therapy.

Attention to the transference relationship and the working alliance are important strategies to gauge and manage the ongoing work with the child and the family. The therapist must address negative transference if present, otherwise the sessions will be unproductive and may be terminated prematurely. Even if addressed, the sessions could be terminated, but in addressing the negative transference it is possible to turn things around. Establishing a strong working alliance with the child and family offers the best safeguards to the security of the therapy; however, this is not always possible and may change over time, despite what may have appeared to be a strong alliance earlier in the therapeutic relationship.

One 8-year-old boy who lived alone with his single mother enjoyed a positive relationship with his male therapist. As the therapy progressed, the boy became increasingly fond of the therapist, developing a father transference. He invited the therapist to his home to attend his birthday party. Here it was

> **Attend to the transference and the working alliance to gauge and manage the ongoing work with the child and family**

Clinical Pearl
Positive Transference Is Not Always Helpful

A positive transference can be helpful to the progress of the therapy. The child or parent may have a highly positive regard for the therapist that is based in part on a transference relationship. It is not necessary to address the positive transference as long as the therapy is progressing and the alliance is intact. However, the therapist must be on guard for unrealistic expectations that could put the therapy at risk.

necessary to address the transference issue: Gently, the boy was helped to recognize the therapist was someone who was helping him with his worries and problems – they had a job to do together. As much as the therapist liked the boy, he could not go to his home and attend his party, because then they would no longer be working together, and the therapist would no longer be his therapist. He could not be his father, or his uncle or big brother, but he could be his therapist. Helping the boy come to terms with the lack of a father formed the next phase in the therapy.

4.5.4   Resistance

Client resistance is a common feature of the therapeutic process. The children/ youths may present themselves as doing much better than they are, denying problems and painting an unrealistically rosy picture. Suspecting that this may be a manifestation of resistance, the clinician should address these issues directly – for example, by saying, "You are telling me that everything is going well, but I can see in your manner that you don't seem to feel that way. I have the impression that it has been difficult for you to talk about some of the things that are bothering you." Pause; wait for the youth to reply. If there is no response, then ask: "What sort of things may make it difficult for you to talk about your true feelings?"

One of the more challenging scenarios arises when the youth and the parents have different points of view on the need for therapy. Sometimes youths will begin therapy because they feel pressured by their parents or because they may want to please them. In these circumstances, avoid the temptation to align with the parents, and instead focus on the predicament in which the youth finds himself/herself and try to identify an issue that the youth will perceive as helpful, yet consistent with your own broad understanding of what will be therapeutic for the youth.

Issues of confidentiality can become a problem in therapy with a youth when the parents anxiously and insistently seek information on their son's/ daughter's progress in treatment. Sometimes the youth may be willing to include the parents in joint sessions, to facilitate direct communication between parents and them. However, the youth may refuse to participate in joint sessions, and the therapist must respect the wishes of the youth. Unless these issues are handled sensitively, therapy can end prematurely.

4.6   Multicultural, Gender, and Social Disadvantage Issues

4.6.1   Gender Issues

Although boys and girls are largely similar in their language development, boys develop language somewhat more slowly, are more likely to have late language emergence, and, depending on the criteria and cutoffs applied, may be somewhat more likely to meet criteria for some language and speech disorders (Law et al., 2000). Gender differences in language development tend to diminish by school age (Bornstein, Hahn, & Haynes, 2004).

Boys with LI are more likely to be referred for intervention than girls with LI (Zhang & Tomblin, 2000). Sex ratios in clinical samples are greater than those in epidemiological studies. Given the large number of unidentified language disorders among clinical populations, it appears that girls with LI are missed, rather than that boys are overdiagnosed.

Relatively few studies have addressed gender issues in the psychosocial outcomes of LI, although psychosocial correlates and outcomes of LI are usually reported separately for boys versus girls. One study of preschool children with LI found a stronger relationship between LI and disruptive behavior and peer problems for boys than for girls (Stowe, Arnold, & Ortiz, 1999). Rates of comorbid emotional and behavioral concerns among children and youth with LI appear to parallel general gender patterns of behavior problems, in which internalizing problems are relatively more common among girls, and externalizing problems are more common among boys (e.g., Keenan & Shaw, 1997; Zahn-Waxler, 1993). Some data suggest that girls with LI are more likely to have emotional concerns and anxiety than boys with LI (e.g., Beitchman et al., 1986); however, LI may exacerbate both internalizing and externalizing difficulties, for both girls and boys.

Research suggests that parents talk more to their daughters than to their sons, which may partly account for gender differences in rates of early language development (Leaper, Anderson, & Sanders, 1998). It is possible that the child's language difficulties may present a more noticeable challenge to parent–child relationships when a daughter's language skills are not strong, as this may represent a greater discrepancy from parental expectations.

Girls with LI appear to have an increased risk of social withdrawal compared with boys with LI. However, due to deviations from social expectations related to gender, it is possible that social withdrawal in boys is also more likely to raise concern than similar behavior in girls. The combination of communication/comprehension difficulties and social withdrawal may result in extremely limited participation at school. Gender impacts may be compounding; research has shown more limited classroom participation and less teacher attention for girls in comparison with boys (Sadker & Sadker, 1994); furthermore, girls are less likely than boys to be referred for intervention.

This combination of limited communication and social withdrawal may also leave girls with LI isolated and vulnerable in areas in addition to academics. Rates of childhood sexual abuse (based on retrospective young adult reports) were up to three times higher among girls with LI than among typical language girls (Brownlie et al., 2007). The prevalence of reported sexual abuse was much lower among male participants and not differentiated by language status. Although LI is often an invisible disability, the associated vulnerability may be perceptible to perpetrators targeting isolated or otherwise vulnerable youths. Gender socialization exacerbates the vulnerability of girls with LI. Young women with LI are also more likely to become parents at an early age (Brownlie, Beitchman, Graham, Schachter, & Mirdha, 2012). Supporting girls with LI in developing confidence and assertiveness may be an important therapeutic goal.

Similarly, boys with LI have specific gender-related vulnerabilities to involvement in delinquency and antisocial behavior (Brownlie et al., 2004). Both academic difficulties and social problems make it more difficult for boys with LI to form friendships with peers who are academically engaged and successful. As a result, boys with LI may become involved with antisocial youths and delinquent activities, in part due to gender norms supporting delinquent and aggressive behavior in young men (Brownlie et al., 2004). Gender norms may compound language difficulties in getting boys, particularly adolescents, with language challenges to engage verbally in treatment.

4.6.2　Bilingual and Multilingual Children

Assessing and treating language development and potential impairment is more complicated for children who are learning multiple languages than children learning a single language. This complexity is increased by variations within bilingual/multilingual groups of children based on the contexts of their language learning. For example, some children learn one language before being introduced to others, perhaps with different individuals speaking each. Often children will speak one language at home and a different language in the community and at school; the vocabularies they learn will reflect those contexts (Hoff, 2006).

Diagnosing LI is complex for the multilingual child. In part this is because research is only beginning to examine typical and atypical language development in multilingual children and the determinants of their language outcomes (Hoff, 2006). Language proficiency in each language is proportional to the amount of exposure in that language. Assessment in one language may underestimate the abilities of multilingual children. In the area of vocabulary, in particular, children may have words for as many concepts as monolingual children, but the words may be in different languages (Hoff, 2006). On the other hand, exposure to multiple languages does not prevent LI; multilingual children with LI may be missed if delays are assumed to be wholly due to their multilanguage status.

In addition, cultural differences also complicate assessment. For example, cultural differences in pragmatics (such as cultural norms against answering obvious questions) and dialect differences may increase risk of inaccurate assessment or bias. Children who speak primarily nonstandard English, such as African American English, risk misdiagnosis if assessed solely using standard English (Hoff, 2006). Assessments of the child's spontaneous speech and measuring the complexity of expressive language (e.g., length and number of unique words per utterance and use of complex sentences) avoids cultural biases and can identify LI (Paul & Norbury, 2012), if the assessment can be done in the child's primary language. In addition, tests of nonword repetition do not appear to be culturally biased.

In addition, the degree of impairment is important to consider in identifying LI in linguistic and cultural contexts other than standard English. If the child's communication is causing difficulties in his or her own cultural context, there is more basis to diagnose a LI. This does not mean that skills in standard English will not be beneficial for most youth in North America; however, understanding deficits to be due to cultural differences or limited exposure rather than LI is crucial for case formulation (Paul & Norbury, 2012).

In addition, there are cultural differences in parenting. High levels of interaction with infants and child-centered speech are typical of middle class North Americans, and predict language development within the North American context. However, other cultures differ in their practices around language acquisition; language development differs but is on the whole robust to these differences (Hoff, 2006). The clinician needs to be sensitive to the parents' cultural practices, while encouraging activities that strongly support language growth, such as book reading. Cultural factors may play a role in responses to suggested treatment approaches especially as they involve parents and family. Emphasis on the particular needs of the child or youth because of their unique language challenges may encourage flexibility in working out a mutually acceptable strategy respecting the family's preferences.

4.6.3   Social Disadvantage

Social disadvantage is consistently associated with poorer language functioning and higher rates of LI. Although genetics may play a role, differences associated with SES can be largely accounted for by differences in parental language use (Hoff, 2006). This is good news, as environmental factors can be amendable with intervention. In addition to differences in education, however, social disadvantage is generally accompanied by psychosocial stressors such as poverty, parent mental health or substance use concerns, and vulnerability to violence and marginalization with fewer resources. Attention to the family context is important to set reasonable expectations so that the family remains engaged in treatment. Attention to the impact on the child is also key; a stressful home environment will compound what is often a stressful school environment. Plans for the child or youth to be involved in an activity in a calm and supportive context may provide relief as well as opportunities for positive interaction with peers and supportive adults.

In addition, greater levels of advocacy may be necessary on behalf of the child or family. For example, some parents may have less comfort or experience navigating educational bureaucracies to try to obtain services on behalf of their child, or may have language or literacy limitations. They may need more specific information on how to go about that process or coaching or assistance in completing it.

5

Further Reading

Hoff, E. (2006). How social contexts support and shape language development. *Developmental Review, 26*(1), 55–88.
  This review provides a detailed examination of the role of environmental factors in language development. The review integrates distinct bodies of research on child, family, community, and broader social factors, and provides excellent information on parenting strategies, peer factors, cultural differences, and development in multilingual children.

Durkin, K., & Conti-Ramsden, G. (2010). Young people with specific language impairment: A review of social and emotional functioning in adolescence. *Child Language Teaching and Therapy, 26*(2), 105–121.
  This paper gives a detailed overview of psychosocial functioning of language-impaired adolescents. The review examines youth outcomes in a developmental context, with a special emphasis on social functioning. Peer relations, bullying, emotional/behavior problems are discussed, as well as implications for service provision.

Johnson, C. J., Beitchman, J. H., & Brownlie, E. B. (2010). Twenty-year follow-up of children with and without speech-language impairments: Family, educational, occupational, and quality of life outcomes. *American Journal of Speech-Language Pathology, 19*(1), 51–65.
  This article reports on life outcomes of childhood language impairment identified in a community sample of children identified with language or speech impairment at age 5. The findings of this study, taken in combination with the broader literature on adult outcomes of language impairment, which is reviewed, provide more detailed information about the prognosis of language impairment.

Friedberg, R. D., McClure, J. M., & Garcia, J. H. (2009). *Cognitive therapy techniques for children and adolescents: Tools for enhancing practice.* New York: Guilford Press.
  This book provides an excellent introduction to the techniques and principles of cognitive behavior therapy with children and youth with a variety of clinical problems. Though not specifically intended for children and youth with language impairments, there are sufficient examples that the practitioner can usefully adapt the techniques described, for the language-impaired client.

Cohen, N. J. (2001). *Language impairment and psychopathology in infants, children, and adolescents.* Thousand Oaks, CA: Sage.
  This book examines language impairment and psychopathology from a developmental perspective, illustrating the many ways in which impaired language and communication are related to social and emotional development. It discusses the interface between language impairment and specific diagnoses, as well as problems with emotional regulation, academic achievement and cognitive development and more.

Shelleby, E. C., Shaw, D. S., Cheong, J., Chang, H., Gardner, F., Dishion, T. J., & Wilson, M. N. (2012). Behavioral control in at-risk toddlers: The influence of the family check-up. *Journal of Clinical Child and Adolescent Psychology, 41*(3), 288–301.
  This article illustrates the importance of proactive parenting in reducing child behavior problems and increasing children's behavioral control. Using family-centered interventions, the authors discuss strategies of greater parental engagement, and prompting and reinforcing positive behaviors which lead to improved adaptation. The principles discussed can be applied to reduce and prevent behavioral problems with young children.

6

References

Achenbach, T. M. (2009). *The Achenbach system of empirically based assessment (ASEBA): Development, findings, theory, and applications.* Burlington, VT: University of Vermont Research Center for Children, Youth and Families.

Adams, C., Baxendale, J., Lloyd, J., & Aldred, C. (2005). Pragmatic language impairment: Case studies of social and pragmatic language therapy. *Child Language Teaching and Therapy, 21,* 227–250.

Alt, M., & Plante, E. (2006). Factors that influence lexical and semantic fast mapping of young children with specific language impairment. *Journal of Speech, Language, and Hearing Research, 49,* 941–954.

American Psychiatric Association. (2000). *Diagnostic and statistical manual of mental disorders* (4th ed., text-revision). Washington, DC: Author.

American Psychiatric Association. (2013). *Diagnostic and statistical manual of mental disorders* (5th ed.). Washington, DC: Author.

Archibald, L. M., & Gathercole, S. E. (2006). Nonword repetition: A comparison of tests. *Journal of Speech, Language, and Hearing Research, 49,* 970–983.

Archibald, L., & Joanisse, M. F. (2009). On the sensitivity and specificity of nonword repetition and sentence recall to language and memory impairments in children. *Journal of Speech, Language, and Hearing Research, 52*(4), 899–914.

Bandura, A. (1973). *Aggression: A social learning analysis.* Englewood Cliffs, NJ: Prentice-Hall.

Bankson, N. W. (1990). *BLT-2: Bankson Language Test* (2nd ed.). Austin, TX: Pro-Ed.

Barrett, S., Prior, M., & Manjiviona, J. (2004). Children on the borderlands of autism: Differential characteristics in social, imaginative, communicative and repetitive behaviour domains. *Autism, 8*(1), 61–87.

Beck, J. S., Beck, A. T., & Jolly, J. B. (2005). *Beck Youth Inventories* (2nd ed.). San Antonio, TX: Pearson.

Becker, J. A., Place, K. S., Tenzer, S. A., & Frueh, B. C. (1991). Teachers' impressions of children varying in pragmatic skills. *Journal of Applied Developmental Psychology, 12*(4), 397–412.

Bedore, L., & Leonard, L. (1998). Specific language impairment and grammatical morphology: A discriminant function analysis. *Journal of Speech, Language, and Hearing Research, 41*(5), 965–1220.

Beitchman, J. H. (1985). Therapeutic considerations with the language-impaired preschool child. *Canadian Journal of Psychiatry, 30*(8), 609–613.

Beitchman, J. H., Brownlie, E. B., Inglis, A., Wild, J., Ferguson, B., Schachter, D., … Mathews, R. (1996). Seven-year follow-up of speech/language impaired and control children: Psychiatric outcome. *Journal of Child Psychology and Psychiatry, 37*(8), 961–970.

Beitchman, J. H., Brownlie, E. B., Inglis, A., Wild, J., Mathews, R., Schachter, D., … Lancee, W. (1994). Seven-year follow-up of speech/language-impaired and control children: Speech/language stability and outcome. *Journal of the American Academy of Child & Adolescent Psychiatry, 33*(9), 1322–1330.

Beitchman, J. H., & Inglis, A. (1991). The continuum of linguistic dysfunction from pervasive developmental disorders to dyslexia. *Psychiatric Clinics of North America, 14*(1), 95–111.

Beitchman, J. H., Jiang, H., Koyama, E., Johnson, C. J., Escobar, M., Atkinson, L., … Vida, R. (2008). Models and determinants of vocabulary growth from kindergarten to adulthood. *Journal of Child Psychology and Psychiatry, 49*(6), 626–634.

Beitchman, J. H., Nair, R., Clegg, M., Ferguson, B, & Patel, P. G. (1986). Prevalence of psychiatric disorders in children with speech and language disorders. *Journal of the American Academy of Child and Adolescent Psychiatry, 25*(4), 528–535.

Beitchman, J. H., Wilson, B., Brownlie, E. B., Walters, H., & Lancee, W. (1996). Long-term consistency in speech/language profiles: I. Developmental and academic outcomes. *Journal of the American Academy of Child and Adolescent Psychiatry, 35*(6), 804–814.

Beitchman, J. H., Wilson, B., Johnson, C. J., Atkinson, L., Young, A., Adlaf, E., … Douglas, L. (2001). Fourteen-year follow-up of speech/language-impaired and control children: Psychiatric outcome. *Journal of the American Academy of Child and Adolescent Psychiatry, 40*(1), 75–82.

Beitchman, J. H., & Young, A. (1997). Learning disorders with a special emphasis on reading disorders: A review of the past 10 years. *Journal of the American Academy of Child and Adolescent Psychiatry, 36*(8), 1020–1032.

Berg, B. (1989). *Drugs and alcohol game.* Los Angeles, CA: Creative Therapy Store.

Berg, B. (1990a). *The anger control game.* Dayton, OH: Cognitive Counseling Resources.

Berg, B. (1990b). *The self-control game.* Dayton, OH: Cognitive Counseling Resources.

Berk, L. E. (1992). Children's private speech. In L. E. Berk & R. M. Diaz (Eds.), *Private speech: From social interaction to self-regulation* (pp. 17–53). Hillsdale, NJ: Erlbaum.

Birmaher, B., Khetarpal, S., Brent, D., Cully, M., Balach, L., Kaufman, J., & McKenzie Neer, S. (1997). The Screen for Child Anxiety Related Emotional Disorders (SCARED): Scale construction and psychometric characteristics. *Journal of the American Academy of Child & Adolescent Psychiatry, 36*(4), 545 -553.

Bishop, D. V. M. (1997). *Uncommon understanding: Development and disorders of language comprehension in children.* Hove, UK: Psychology Press.

Bishop, D. V. M. (2003). *Children's Communication Checklist – 2 (CCC-2)* London: Psychological Corporation.

Bishop, D. V. M. (2006). What causes specific language impairment in children? *Current Directions in Psychological Science, 15*(5), 217–221.

Bishop, D. V. M., Hardiman, M. J., & Barry, J. G. (2012). Auditory deficit as a consequence rather than endophenotype of specific language impairment: Electrophysiological evidence. *PLoS ONE, 7*(5): e35851. doi:10.1371/journal.pone.0035851

Bishop, D. V. M., & McDonald, D. (2009). Identifying language impairment in children: Combining language test scores with parental report. *International Journal of Language & Communication Disorders, 44*, 600–615.

Bishop, D. V. M., & Hayiou-Thomas, M. E. (2008). Heritability of specific language impairment depends on diagnostic criteria. *Genes, Brain and Behavior, 7*(3), 365–372.

Bishop, D. V. M., & Norbury, C. F. (2002). Exploring the borderlands of autistic disorder and specific language impairment: A study using standardized diagnostic instruments. *Journal of Child Psychology & Psychiatry & Allied Disciplines, 43*, 917-929.

Bishop, D. V. M., North, T., & Donlan, C. (1995). Genetic basis of specific language impairment: Evidence from a twin study. *Developmental Medicine and Child Neurology, 37*(1), 56–71.

Bloom, L., & Lahey, M. (1978). *Language development and language disorders.* Somerset, NJ: John Wiley.

Boehm, A. (2000). *Boehm Test of Basic Concepts* (3rd ed.) San Antonia, TX: Pearson.

Bornstein, M., H., Hahn, C.-S., & Haynes, O. M. (2004). Specific and general language performance across early childhood: Stability and gender considerations. *First Language, 24*(3), 267–305.

Botting, N., & Conti-Ramsden, G. (1999). Pragmatic language impairment without autism. *Autism, 3*, 371–396.

Bowers, L., Huisingh, R., LoGiudice, C., & Orman, J. (2010). *The Expressive Language Test 2.* East Moline, IL: LinguiSystems.

Bracken, B. A. (2006). *Bracken Basic Concept Scale: Expressive* (3rd ed.). San Antonio, TX: Pearson.

Brackenbury, T., & Pye, C. (2005). Semantic deficits in children with language impairments: Issues for clinical assessment. *Language, Speech & Hearing Services in Schools, 36*(1), 5–16.

Breslau, N., Dickens, W. T., Flynn, J., R., Peterson, E. L., & Lucia, V. C. (2007). Low birthweight and social disadvantage: Tracking their relationship with children's IQ during the period of school attendance. *Intelligence, 34*(4), 351–362.

Brinton, B., & Fujiki, M. (2006). Social intervention for children with language impairment: Factors affecting efficacy. *Communication Disorders Quarterly, 28*(1), 39–41.

Brownlie, E. B., Beitchman, J. H., Escobar, M., Young, A., Atkinson, L., Johnson, C.,... Douglas, L. (2004). Early language impairment and young adult delinquent and aggressive behavior. *Journal of Abnormal Child Psychology, 32*(4), 453–467.

Brownlie, E. B., Beitchman, J. H., Graham, E., Schachter, D., & Mirdha, N. (2012). *Gender and transitions to adulthood among emerging adults with childhood language impairment: Results of a 25-year longitudinal study.* Poster presentation. Canadian Psychological Association Annual Convention, Halifax, Nova Scotia, Canada, June, 2012.

Brownlie, E. B., Jabbar, A., Beitchman, J., Vida, R., & Atkinson, L. (2007). Language impairment and sexual assault of girls and women: Findings from a community sample. *Journal of Abnormal Psychology, 35*(4), 618–626.

Buckley, J. A., & Epstein, M. H. (2004). The Behavioral and Emotional Rating Scale-2 (BERS-2): Providing a comprehensive approach to strength-based assessment. *The California School Psychologist, 9,* 21–27.

Carrow-Woolfolk, E. (1999a). *Comprehensive Assessment of Spoken Language (CASL).* Circle Pines, MN: American Guidance Services.

Carrow-Woolfolk, E. (1999b). *Test for Auditory Comprehension of Language* (3rd ed.). Austin, TX: Pro-Ed.

Carrow-Woolfolk, E. (2011). *OWLS II: Oral and written language skills* (2nd ed.). Torrance, CA: Western Psychological Services.

Catts, H. W., Fey, M. E., Zhang, X., & Tomblin, J. B. (1999). Language basis of reading and reading disabilities: Evidence from a longitudinal investigation. *Scientific Studies of Reading, 3*(4), 331–361.

Chen, K. (2006). Social skills intervention for students with emotional/behavioral disorders: A literature review from the American perspective. *Educational Research and Reviews, 1*(3), 143–149.

Chiat, S. & Roy, P. (2007). The preschool repetition test: An evaluation of performance in typically developing and clinically referred children. *Journal of Speech, Language, and Hearing Research, 50,* 429–443.

Choi, D. H., & Kim, J. (2003). Practicing social skills training for young children with low peer acceptance: A cognitive-social learning model. *Early Childhood Education Journal, 31*(1), 41–46.

Cohen, N. J. (2001). *Language impairment and psychopathology in infants, children, and adolescents.* Thousand Oaks, CA: Sage.

Cohen, N. J., Davine, M., Horodezky, N., Lipsett, L., & Isaacson, L. (1993). Unsuspected language impairment in psychiatrically disturbed children: Prevalence and language and behavioral characteristics. *Journal of the American Academy of Child & Adolescent Psychiatry, 32*(3), 595–603.

Cohen, N. J., Menna, R., Vallance, D. D., Barwick, M. A., Im, N., & Horodezky, N. B. (1998). Language, social cognitive processing, and behavioral characteristics of psychiatrically disturbed children with previously identified and unsuspected language impairments. *Journal of Child Psychology and Psychiatry, 39*(6), 853–864.

Cohen, N. J., Vallance, D. D., Barwick, M., Im, N., Menna, R., Horodezky, N. B., & Isaacson, L. (2000). The interface between ADHD and language impairment: An examination of language, achievement, and cognitive processing. *Journal of Child Psychology and Psychiatry, 41*(3), 353–362.

Conners, C. K. (1997). *Manual for the Conners' Rating Scales* (revised). North Tonawanda, NY: Multi- Health Systems.

Conti-Ramsden, G. M. (2003). Processing and linguistic markers in young children with specific language impairment (SLI). *Journal of Speech, Language, and Hearing Research, 46(5)*, 1029-37.

Conti-Ramsden, G. M., & Botting, N. F. (1999). Classification of children with specific language impairment: Longitudinal considerations. *Journal of Speech, Language and Hearing Research, 42*(5), 1195–1204.

Conti-Ramsden, G. M., & Botting, N. F. (2004). Characteristics of children with specific language impairment. In L. Verhoeven & H. van Balkom (Eds.), *Classification of developmental language disorders* (pp. 23–39). Mahwah, NJ: Erlbaum.

Conti-Ramsden, G. & Durkin, K. (2012). Language development and assessment in the preschool period. *Neuropsychology Review, 22*, 384–401.

Crais, E. (2011). Testing and beyond: Strategies and tools for evaluation and assessment of infants and toddlers. *Language, Speech, Hearing in Schools, 42*, 341–346.

DeCasper, A. J., & Fifer, W. P. (1980). Of human bonding: Newborns prefer their mothers' voices. *Science, 208*(44), 1174–1176.

Delonia, J., & Pettigrew, C. (1998). *Effects of the modeling of verbal and nonverbal procedures for interactions with peers through social stories and scaffolded activities on social competence of 3- and 4-year-old children with specific language impairments.* Houston, TX: Texas Woman's University.

de Ridder, H., & van der Stege, H. (2004). Early detection of developmental language disorders. In L. Verhoeven & H. van Balkom (Eds.), *Classification of developmental language disorders: Theoretical issues and clinical implications* (pp. 137–158). Mahwah, NJ: Erlbaum.

DeThorne, L. S., & Watkins R. V. (2001). Listeners' perceptions of language use in children. *Language Speech and Hearing Services in Schools, 23*(3), 142–148.

Diaz, R. M., & Berk, L. E. (Eds.). (1992). *Private speech: From social interaction to self-regulation.* Hillsdale, NJ: Erlbaum.

Dionne, G., Dale, P. S., Boivin, M., & Plomin, R. (2003). Genetic evidence for bidirectional effects of early lexical and grammatical development. *Child Development, 74*(2), 394–412.

Dunn, L. M., & Dunn, D. M. (2007). *Peabody Picture Vocabulary Test* (4th ed.). San Antonio, TX: Pearson.

Durkin, K., & Conti-Ramsden, G. (2010). Young people with specific language impairment: A review of social and emotional functioning in adolescence. *Child Language Teaching and Therapy, 26*(2), 105–121.

Elliott, S. N., & Busse, R. T. (1991). Social skills assessment and intervention with children and adolescents: Guidelines for assessment and training procedures. *School Psychology International, 12*(1-2), 63–83.

Ellis, L. (2011). Fostering resiliency using a strengths-based approach. *Research Bytes No. 1.* Retrieved from http://www.mtroyal.ca/wcm/groups/public/documents/pdf/strengthsbasedapproachrb.pdf

Ellis, E. M., & Thal, D. J. (2008). Early language delay and risk for language impairment. *Perspectives on Language Learning and Education, 15*(3), 93–100.

Epstein, M. H. (2004). *BERS-2: Behavioral and Emotional Rating Scale* (2nd ed.). Austin, TX: Pro-Ed.

Epstein, M. H., & Sharma, J. (1998). *Behavioral and emotional rating scale: A strength-based approach to assessment.* Austin, TX: PRO-ED.

Eriksson, M., Westerlund, M. & Miniscalco, C. (2010). Problems and limitations in studies on screening for language delay. *Research in Developmental Disabilities, 31*, 943–950.

Fava, E., Hull, R., & Bortfeld, H. (2011). Linking behavioral and neurophysiological indicators of perceptual tuning to language. *Frontiers in Psychology, 2,* 174. doi:10.3389/fpsyg.2011.00174

Fenson, L., Dale, P. S., Reznick, J. S., Bates, E., Thal, D. J., & Pethick, S. J. (1994). Variability in early communicative development. *Monographs of the Society for Research in Child Development, 59*(5), v–173.

Fenson, L., Dale, P. S., Reznick, J. S., Thal, D., Bates, E., Hartung, J. P., ... Reilly, J. S. (1993). *The MacArthur Communicative Development Inventories: User's guide and technical manual.* San Diego, CA: Singular.

Fey, M. E., Long, S. H., & Cleave, P. L. (1994). Reconsideration of IQ criteria in the definition of specific language impairment. In: R. V. Watkins & M. L. Rice (Eds.), *Specific language impairments in children* (pp. 161–178). Baltimore, MD: Brookes.

Fey, M. E., Richard, G. J., Geffner, D., Kamhi, A. G., Medwetsky, L., Paul, D., ... Schooling, T. (2011). Auditory processing disorder and auditory/language interventions: An evidence-based systematic review. *Language, Speech, and Hearing Services in Schools, 42*(3), 246–264.

Fey, M. E., Warren, S. F., Brady, N., Finestack, L. H., Bredin-Oja, S. L., Fairchild, M., ... Yoder, P. J. (2006). Early effects of responsivity education/prelinguistic milieu teaching for children with developmental delays and their parents. *Journal of Speech, Language, and Hearing Research, 49*(3), 526–547.

Friedberg, R. D., McClure, J. M., & Garcia, J. H. (2009). *Cognitive therapy techniques for children and adolescents: Tools for enhancing practice.* New York: Guilford Press.

Fujiki, M., Brinton, B., Morgan, M., & Hart, C. G. (1999). Withdrawn and sociable behavior in children with language impairment. *Language, Speech, and Hearing Services in Schools, 30*(2), 183–195.

Furlong, M., MicGilloway, S., Bywater, T., Hutchings, J., Smith, S. M., & Donnelly, M. (2012). Group parenting programmes for improving behavioural problems in children aged 3 to 12 years. *Cochrane Database of Systematic Reviews, 2,* CD008225. doi:10.1002/14651858.CD008225.pub2

Gallagher, T. M. (1999). Interrelationships among children's language, behavior, and emotional problems. *Topics in Language Disorders, 19*(2), 1–15.

Ganger, J., & Brent, M. (2004). Reexamining the vocabulary spurt. *Developmental Psychology, 40*(4), 621–632.

Gardner, R. A. (1973). *The talking, feeling, and doing game.* Cresskill, NJ: Creative Therapeutics.

Gardner, R. A. (1998). *The helping, sharing, and caring game.* Plainview, NY: Childswork, Childsplay.

Gathercole, S. E., & Baddeley, A. D. (1996). *Children's Test of Nonword Repetition.* London: Pearson Assessment.

Gershkoff-Stowe, L., & Hahn, E. R. (2007). Fast mapping skills in the developing lexicon. *Journal of Speech, Language, and Hearing Research, 50*(3), 682–697.

Giddan, J. J., Milling, L., & Campbell, N. B. (1996). Unrecognized language and speech deficits in preadolescent psychiatric inpatients. *American Journal of Orthopsychiatry, 66*(1), 85–92.

Gillam, R. B., & Hoffman, L. M. (2004). Information processing in children with specific language impairment. In L. Verhoeven & H. van Balkom (Eds.), *Classification of developmental language disorders: Theoretical issues and clinical implications* (pp. 137–158). Mahwah, NJ: Erlbaum.

Gilliam, J. E., & Miller, L. (2006). *Pragmatic Language Skills Inventory.* Austin, TX: Pro-Ed.

Glascoe, F. P. (1997). *Parents' Evaluation of Developmental Status* (PEDS). Nashville, TN: Ellsworth & Vandermeer Press.

Glascoe, F. P., & Leew, S. (2010). Parenting behaviors, perceptions, and psychosocial risk: Impacts on young children's development. *Pediatrics, 125*(2), 213–319.

Goldstein, A. P., Click, B., & Gibbs, J. C. (1998). *Aggression Replacement Training: A comprehensive intervention for aggressive youth.* Champaign, IL: Research Press.

Goldstein, A. P., Spranfkin, R. P., Gershaw, N. J., & Klein, P. (1979). *Skillstreaming the adolescent.* Champaign, IL: Research Press.

Guralnick, M. J., & Neville, B. (1997). Designing early intervention programs to promote children's social competence. In M. J. Guralnick (Ed.), *The effectiveness of early intervention* (pp. 579–610). Baltimore, MD: Brookes.

Hammill, D. D., Brown, V. L., Larsen, S. C., & Wiederholt, J. L. (2007). *Test of Adolescent and Adult Language* (4th ed.). Austin, TX: Pro-Ed.

Hammill, D. D., Mather, N., & Roberts, R. (2001). *Illinois Test of Psycholinguistic Abilities* (3rd ed.). Austin TX: Pro-Ed.

Hammill, D. D., & Newcomer, P. L. (2008a). *Test of Language Development - Intermediate* (4th ed.). Austin TX: Pro-Ed.

Hammill, D. D., & Newcomer, P. L. (2008b). *Test of Language Development - Primary* (4th ed.). Austin TX: Pro-Ed.

Hammill, D. D., & Newcomer, P. I. (2009). *Pragmatic Language Observation Scale.* Austin, TX: Hammill Institute on Disabilities.

Hart, B., & Risley, T. R. (1995). *Meaningful differences in the everyday experience of young American children.* Baltimore, MD: Brookes.

Hemmeter, M. L., Ostrosky, M., & Fox, L. (2006). Social and emotional foundations for early learning: A conceptual model for intervention. *School Psychology Review, 35*(4), 583–601.

Hoff, E. (2006). How social contexts support and shape language development. *Developmental Review, 26*(1), 55–88.

Hresko, W. P., Reid, K. D., & Hammill, D. D. (1991). *TELD 3: Test of Early Language Development* (3rd ed.). Austin, TX: Pro-Ed.

In-Albon, T., & Schneider, S. (2007). Psychotherapy of childhood anxiety disorders: A meta-analysis. *Psychotherapy and Psychosomatics, 76*(1), 15–24.

Johnson, C. J., Beitchman, J. H., & Brownlie, E. B. (2010). Twenty-year follow-up of children with and without speech-language impairments: Family, educational, occupational, and quality of life outcomes. *American Journal of Speech-Language Pathology, 19*(1), 51–65.

Johnson, C. J., Beitchman, J. H., Young, A., Escobar, M., Atkinson, L., Wilson, B., … Wang, M. (1999). Fourteen-year follow-up of children with and without speech/language impairments: Speech/language stability and outcomes. *Journal of Speech, Language, and Hearing Research, 42*(3), 744–760.

Jones, R. N., Sheridan, S. N., & Binns, W. R. (1993). Schoolwide social skills training: Providing preventive services to students at-risk. *School Psychology Quarterly, 8*(1), 57–80. Retrieved from http://www.eric.ed.gov/ERICWebPortal/search/detailmini.jsp?_nfpb=true&_&ERICExtSearch_SearchValue_0=EJ484551&ERICExtSearch_SearchType_0=no&accno=EJ484551

Kahneman, D. (2011). *Thinking fast and slow.* New York: Farrar, Straus, and Giroux.

Kamhi, A. G. (1998). Trying to make sense of developmental language disorders. *Language, Speech, and Hearing Services in Schools, 29*(1), 35–44.

Kamhi, A. G., Masterson, J., & Apel, K. (Eds.). (2007). *Clinical decision making in developmental language disorders.* Baltimore, MD: Brookes.

Kavale, K. A., & Mostert, M. P. (2004). Social skills interventions for individuals with learning disabilities. *Learning Disability Quarterly, 27*(1), 31–43.

Keenan, K., & Shaw, D. (1997). Developmental and social influences on young girls' early problem behavior. *Psychological Bulletin, 121*(1), 95–113.

Kendall, P. C., & Suveg, S. (2006). Treating anxiety disorders in youth. In P. C. Kendall (Ed.), *Child and adolescent therapy: Cognitive-behavioral procedures* (3rd ed., pp. 243–294). New York: Guildford Press.

Klee, T., Carson, D. K., Gavin, W. J., Hall, L., Kent, A., & Reece, S. (1998). Concurrent and predictive validity of an early language screening program. *Journal of Speech, Language, and Hearing Research, 41,* 627–641.

Kovacs, M. (2010). *Children's Depression Inventory* (2nd ed.) San Antonio, TX: Pearson.

Langberg, J. M., & Becker, S. P. (2012). Does long-term medication use improve the academic outcomes of youth with attention-deficit/hyperactivity disorder? *Clinical Child and Family Psychology Review.* doi:10.1007/s10567-012-0117-8

Lavigne, M. & Van Rybroek, G. (2010). Breakdown in the language zone: The prevalence of language impairments among juvenile and adult offenders and why it matters (University of Wisconsin Legal Studies Research Paper No. 1127). Retrieved from http://ssrn.com/abstract=1663805

Law, J., Boyle, J., Harris, F., Harkness, A., & Nye, C. (2000). Prevalence and natural history of primary speech and language delay: Findings from a systematic review of the literature. *International Journal of Language and Communication Disorders, 35*(2), 165–188.

Law, J., Boyle, J., Harris, F., Harkness, A., & Nye, C. (2000). The feasibility of universal screening for primary speech and language delay: Findings from a systematic review of the literature. *Developmental Medicine & Child Neurology, 42*, 190–200.

Law, J., Garrett, Z., & Nye, C. (2004). The efficacy of treatment for children with developmental speech and language delay/disorder: A meta-analysis. *Journal of Speech, Language, and Hearing Research, 47*(4), 924–943.

Leaper, C., Anderson, K. J., & Sanders, P. (1998). Moderators of gender effects on parents' talk to their children: A meta-analysis. *Developmental Psychology, 34*(1), 3–27.

Leonard, L. B., Deever, P., Miller, C. A., Charest, M., Kurtz, R., & Rauf, L. (2003). The use of grammatical morphemes reflecting aspect and modality by children with specific language impairment. *Journal of Child Language, 30*(4), 769–795.

Leonard, L. B., Weismer, S. E., Miller, C. A., Francis, D. J., Tomblin, J. B., & Kail, R. V. (2007). Speed of processing, working memory, and language impairment in children. *Journal of Speech, Language, and Hearing Research, 50*(2), 408–428.

Leonard, M. A., Milich, R., & Lorch, E. P. (2011). The role of pragmatic language use in mediating the relation between hyperactivity and inattention and social skills problems. *Journal of Speech, Language and Hearing Research, 54*, 567.

Le Paro, K. M., Justice, L., Skibbe, L., & Pianta, R. C. (2004). Relations among maternal, child, and demographic factors and the persistence of preschool language impairment. *American Journal of Speech-Language Pathology, 13*(4), 291–303.

Lewis, B. A., & Thompson, L. A. (1992). A study of developmental speech and language disorders in twins. *Journal of Speech and Hearing Research, 35*(5), 1086–1094.

Leyfer, O., Tager-Flusberg, H., Dowd, M., Tomblin, J. B., & Folstein, S. E. (2008). Overlap between autism and specific language impairment: Comparison of Autism Diagnostic Interview and Autism Diagnostic Observation Schedule scores. *Autism Research, 1*(5), 284–296.

Linseisen, T. (2006). Effective interventions for youth with oppositional defiant disorder. In C. Franklin, M. B. Harris, & P. Allen-Meares (Eds.), *The school services sourcebook: A guide for school professionals* (pp. 57–67). New York: Oxford University Press.

Lovett, M. W., Barron, R. W., & Benson, N. J. (2003). Effective remediation of word identification and decoding difficulties in school-age children with reading disabilities. In H. L. Swanson, K. Harris, & S. Graham (Eds.), *Handbook of learning disabilities* (pp. 273–291). New York: Guilford Press.

Lynam, D., Moffitt, T., & Stouthamer-Loeber, M. (1993). Explaining the relation between IQ and delinquency: Class, race, test motivation, school failure, or self-control? *Journal of Abnormal Psychology, 102*(2), 187–196.

Manassis, K., Tannock, R., Garland, E. J., Minde, K., McInnes, A., & Clarke, S. (2007). The sounds of silence: Language, cognition, and anxiety in selective mutism. *Journal of the American Academy of Child and Adolescent Psychiatry, 46*(9), 1187–1195.

Manolson, H. A. (1979). Parent training: A means of implementing pragmatics in early language remediation. *Human Communication, 4*(2), 275-281.

Masten, A. S., Burt, K. B., Roisman, G. I., Obradovic, J., Long, J. D., & Tellegen, A. (2004). Resources and resilience in the transition to adulthood: Continuity and change. *Development and Psychopathology, 16*(4), 1071–1094.

Moffitt, T. E. (1993). The neuropsychology of conduct disorder. *Development and Psychopathology, 5*, 135–151.

Molina, B. S. G., Hinhsaw, S. P., Swanson, J. M., Arnold, L. E., Vitiello, B., Jenson, P. S., … MTA Cooperative Group. (2009). MTA at 8 years: Prospective follow-up of children treated for combined-type ADHD in a multisite study. *Journal of American Academy of Child & Adolescent Psychiatry, 48*(5), 484–500.

Muris, P. (1997). *The Screen for Child Anxiety Related Emotional Disorders* (revised). Maastricht, The Netherlands: Maastricht University, Department of Psychology.

Muris, P., Mayer, B., Bartelds, E., Tierney, S., & Bogie, N. (1997). The revised version of the Screen for Child Anxiety Related Emotional Disorders (SCARED-R): Treatment sensitivity in an early intervention trial for childhood anxiety disorders. *British Journal of Clinical Psychology, 40*(3), 323-36.

National Literacy Trust. (2010). Management summary of qualitative research report prepared for the face to face research project. Retrieved from http://www.eric.ed.gov. myaccess.library.utoronto.ca/PDFS/ED515953.pdf

Nelson, W. M., & Finch, A. J. (2000). *Children's Inventory of Anger.* Torrance, CA: Western Psychological Services.

Nelson, H. D., Nygren, P., Walker, M., & Panoscha, R. (2006). Screening for speech and language delay in preschool children: Systematic evidence review for the US Preventive Services Task Force. *Pediatrics, 117*(6), 2336–2337.

Nippold, M. A. (2012). Stuttering and language ability in children: Questioning the connection. *American Journal of Speech-language Pathology, 21*(3), 183–196A.

Patterson, G. R., DeBaryshe, B. D., & Ramsey, E. (1989). A developmental perspective on antisocial behavior. *American Psychologist, 44*(2), 329–335.

Paul, R., & Norbury, C. F. (2012). *Language disorders from infancy through adolescence: Listening, speaking, reading, writing, and communicating.* St. Louis, MI: Elsevier.

Pennington, B. F., & Bishop, D. V. M. (2009). Relations among speech, language, and reading disorders. *Annual Review of Psychology, 60*(1), 283–306.

Phelps-Terasaki, D., & Phelps-Gunn, T. (2007). *Test of Pragmatic Language* (2nd Ed.). Austin, TX: Pro-Ed.

Prelock, P. A., Hutchins, T., & Glascoe, F. P. (2008). Speech-language impairment: How to identify the most common and least diagnosed disability of childhood. *Medscape Journal of Medicine, 10*, 136.

Rapee, R. M., Schniering, C. A., & Hudson, J. L. (2009). Anxiety disorders during childhood and adolescence: Origins and treatment. *Annual Review of Clinical Psychology, 5*, 311–341.

Rapin, I., & Allen, A. (1987). *Developmental dysphasia and autism in preschool children: Characteristics and subtypes.* Paper presented at the First International Symposium on Specific Speech and Language Disorders (AFASIC), Reading, England.

Rapin, I. & Dunn, M. (2003). Update on the language disorders of individuals on the autistic spectrum. *Brain & Development, 25*, 166–172.

Redmond, S. M., & Rice, M. L. (1998). The socioemotional behaviors of children with SLI: Social adaptation or social deviance? *Journal of Speech and Hearing Research, 41*(3), 688–700.

Rescorla, L. (1989). The Language Development Survey: A screening tool for delayed language in toddlers. *Journal of Speech and Hearing Disorders, 54*, 587–599.

Rescorla, L. (2005). Age 13 language and reading outcomes in late-talking toddlers. *Journal of Speech, Language, and Hearing Research, 48*(2), 459–472.

Rescorla, L. (2009). Age 17 language and reading outcomes in late-talking toddlers: Support for a dimensional perspective on language delay. *Journal of Speech, Language, and Hearing Research, 52*(1), 16–30.

Reynolds, C. R., & Richmond, B. O. (2008). *Revised Children's Manifest Anxiety Scale* (2nd ed.). Torrance, CA: Western Psychological Services.

Rice, M. L., Hadley, P. A., & Alexander, A. L. (1993). Social biases toward children with speech and language impairments: A correlative causal model of language limitations. *Applied Psycholinguistics, 14*(4), 445–471.

Rice, M. L., Oetting, J. B., Marquis, J., Bode, J., & Pae, S. (1994). Frequency of input effects on word comprehension of children with specific language impairment. *Journal of Speech and Hearing Research, 37*(1), 106–122.

Rice, M. L., Taylor, C. I., & Zubrick, S. R. (2008). Language outcomes of 7-year-old children with and without a history of late language emergence at 24 months. *Journal of Speech, Language, and Hearing Research, 51*, 394-407.

Rice, M. L, & Wexler, K. (1996). Toward tense as a clinical marker of specific language impairment in English-speaking children. *Journal of Speech, Language, and Hearing Research, 39*(6), 1239–1250.

Ronan, K. R., Kendall, P. C., & Rowe, M. (1994). Negative affectivity in children: Development and validation of a self-statement questionnaire. *Cognitive Therapy and Research, 18*(6), 509-528.

Roos, M., & Weismer, S. E. (2008). Language outcomes of late talking toddlers at preschool and beyond. *Perspectives on Language Learning and Education, 15*(3), 119–126.

Rovers, M. M., Schilder, A. G. M., Zielhuis, G. A., & Rosenfeld, R. M. (2004). Otitis media. *The Lancet, 363*(9414), 1080.

Rutter, M., Maughan, B., Meyer, J., Pickles, A., Silberg, J., Simonoff, E., & Taylor, E. (1997). Heterogeneity of antisocial behavior: Causes, continuities, and consequences. In D. A. Hope (Series Ed.) & D. W. Osgood (Vol. Ed.), *Nebraska symposium on motivation: Vol. 44. Motivation & Delinquency* (pp. 45–118). Lincoln, NE: University of Nebraska Press.

Sachse, S., & Suchodoletz, W. (2008). Early identification of language delay by direct language assessment or parent report? *Journal of Developmental & Behavioral Pediatrics, 29*, 34–41.

Sadker, M., & Sadker, D. (1994). *Failing at fairness: How America's schools cheat girls.* New York: Simon & Schuster.

Sax, N., & Weston, E. (eds.). (2007). *Language development milestones.* Retrieved from http://www.rehabmed.ualberta.ca/spa/phonology/milestones.pdf

Schniering, C. A., & Rapee, R. M. (2002). Development and validation of a measure of children's automatic thoughts: The Children's Automatic Thoughts Scale. *Behaviour Research and Therapy, 40*(9), 1091–1109.

Seeff-Gabriel, B., Chiat, S. & Roy, P. (2008). Early Repetition Battery. London: Pearson Education, Inc.

Semel, E., Wiig, E. H., & Secord, W. A. (2003). *CELF-4: Clinical Evaluation of Language Fundamentals* (4th ed.). San Antonio, TX: Pearson.

Semel, E., Wiig, E. H., & Secord, W. A. (2004). *Clinical Evaluation of Language Fundamentals: Screening test (CELF-4 screening test).* Toronto, Canada: The Psychological Corporation.

Seymour, H. N., Roeper, T. W., & de Villiers, J. (2005). *Diagnostic Evaluation of Language Variation (DELV) Norm-referenced.* San Antonio, TX: Pearson.

Shapiro, L. E. (2007). *Dr. Playwell's best behavior game.* Woodbury, NY: Childswork/Childsplay.

Shelleby, E. C., Shaw, D. S., Cheong, J., Chang, H., Gardner, F., Dishion, T. J., … Wilson, M. N. (2012). Behavioral control in at-risk toddlers: The influence of the family checkup. *Journal of Clinical Child and Adolescent Psychology, 41*(3), 288–301.

Smith, G. (2010). *Raine ADHD Study: Long-term outcomes associated with stimulant medication in the treatment of ADHD in children.* Government of Western Australia, Department of Health. Retrieved from http://www.health.wa.gov.au/publications/documents/MICADHD_Raine_ADHD_Study_report_022010.pdf

Snow, P. & Powell, M. (2012). Youth (in)justice: Oral language competence in early life and risk for engagement in antisocial behavior in adolescence. *Trends & Issues in Crime and Criminal Justice, 435*, 1–6.

Snowling, M., Bishop, D. V. M., & Stothard, S. E. (2000). Is preschool language impairment a risk factor for dyslexia in adolescence? *Journal of Child Psychology and Psychiatry, 41*(5), 587–600.

Spence, S. H. (2003). Social skills training with children and young people: Theory, evidence, and practice. *Child and Adolescent Mental Health, 8*(2), 84–96.

Stowe, R. M., Arnold, D. H., & Ortiz, C. (1999). Gender differences in the relationship of language development to disruptive behavior and peer relationships in preschoolers. *Journal of Applied Developmental Psychology, 20*(4), 521–536.

Streng, I. (2008). Using therapeutic board games to promote child mental health. *Journal of Public Health, 7*(4), 4–16.

Sturm, A., & Johnston, J. (1999). Thinking out loud: An exploration of problem-solving language in preschoolers with and without language impairment. *International Journal of Language and Communication Disorders, 34*(1), 1–15.

Sturner, R. A., Kunze, L., Funk, S. G., & Green, J. A. (1993). Elicited imitation: Its effectiveness for speech and language screening. *Developmental Medicine and Child Neurology, 35*(8), 715–726.

Swanson, J. M. (2011). *The SNAP-IV teacher and parent rating scale*. Retrieved from http://www.adhd.net/snap-iv-form.pdf

Teheri, A. & Perry, A. (2012). Exploring the proposed DSM-5 criteria in a clinical sample. *Journal of Autism and Developmental Disorders, 42*(9),1810–1817.

Tomblin, J. B., & Buckwalter, P. (1994). Studies of the genetics of specific language impairment. In R. Watkins & M. Rice (Eds.), *Specific language impairments in children* (pp. 17–34). Baltimore, MD: Brookes.

Tomblin, J. B., Zhang, X., Buckwalter, P., & O'Brien, M. (2003). The stability of primary language disorder: Four years after kindergarten diagnosis. *Journal of Speech, Language and Hearing Research, 46*(6), 1283–1296.

Vallance, D. D., Im, N., & Cohen, N. J. (1999). Discourse deficits associated with psychiatric disorders and with language impairments in children. *Journal of Child Psychology and Psychiatry, 40*(5), 693–704.

van Balkom, H., van Daal, J., & Verhoeven, L. (2004). Subtypes of severe speech and language impairments: Psychometric evidence from 4-year-old children in the Netherlands. *Journal of Speech, Language, and Hearing Research, 47*(6), 1411–1423.

van Daal, J., Verhoeven, L., van Leeuwe, J., & van Balkom, H. (2008). Working memory limitations in children with severe language impairment. *Journal of Communication Disorders, 41*(2), 85–107.

Vaughn, S., Kim, A. H., Sloan, C. M., Hughes, M., Elbaum, B., & Sridhar, D. (2003). Social skills interventions for young children with disabilities: A synthesis of group design studies. *Remedial and special education, 24*(1), 2–15.

Voci, S. C., Beitchman, J. H., Brownlie, E. B., & Wilson, B. (2006). Social anxiety in late adolescence: The importance of early childhood language impairment. *Journal of Anxiety Disorders, 20*(7), 915–930.

Vygotsky, L. S. (1962). *Thought and language*. Cambridge, MA: MIT Press.

Walker, H. M., Colvin, G., & Ramsey, E. (1995). *Antisocial behavior in school: Strategies and best practices*. Pacific Grove, CA: Brooks/Cole.

Walkup, J. T., Albano, A. M., Piacentini, J., Birmaher, B., Compton, S. N., Sherill, J. T., … Kendall, P. C. (2008). Cognitive behavioral therapy, sertraline, or a combination in childhood anxiety. *New England Journal of Medicine, 359*(26), 2753–2766.

Warr-Leeper, G., Wright, N. A., & Mack, A. (1994). Language disabilities of antisocial boys in residential treatment. *Behavioral Disorders, 19*(3), 159–169.

Watson, S. M. R., Richels, C., Michalek, A. P., & Raymer, A. (2012). Psychosocial treatments for ADHD: A systematic appraisal of the evidence. *Journal of Attention Disorders*. Advance online publication. doi:10.1177/1087054712447857

Weismer, S. E. (2007). Typical talkers, late talkers, and children with specific language impairment: A language endowment spectrum? In R. Paul (Ed.), *Language disorders from a developmental perspective* (pp. 83–102). Mahwah, NJ: Erlbaum.

Weisz, J. R., & Bearman, S. K. (2008). Psychological treatments: Overview and critical issues for the field. In M. Rutter, D. Bishop, D. Pine, S. Scott, J. Stevenson, E. Taylor, & A. Thapar (Eds.), *Rutter's child and adolescent psychiatry* (5th ed., pp. 251–268). Oxford: Wiley.

Werry, J. S., Elkind, G. S., & Reeves, J. C. (1987). Attention deficit, conduct, oppositional, and anxiety disorders in children: III. Laboratory differences. *Journal of Abnormal Child Psychology, 15*(3), 409–428.

Whitehouse, A. J. O., Barry, J. G., & Bishop, D. V. M. (2008). Further defining the language impairment of autism: Is there a specific language impairment subtype? *Journal of Communication Disorders, 41*(4), 319–336.

Whitehouse, A. J. O., Robinson, M., & Zubrick, S. R. (2011). Late talking and the risk for psychosocial problems during childhood and adolescence. *Pediatrics, 128*(2), e324–e332.

Wilde, J. (1990). *Let's get rational*. East Troy, WI: LGR Productions.

Williams, D. L. (2010). *Developmental language disorders: Learning language and the brain*. San Diego, CA: Plural.

Wolff, R,, Hommerich, J., Riemsma, R., Antes, G., Lange, S., & Kleijnen, J. (2010). Hearing screening in newborns. *Archives of Diseases of Childhood, 95*, 130–135.

Wood, C. W. (2007). Facilitation of early communicative behaviors. In A. Kamhi, J. Masterston, & K. Apel (Eds.), *Clinical decision making in developmental language disorders* (pp. 121–142). Baltimore, MD: Brookes.

World Health Organization. (1992). *International statistical classification of diseases and related health problems* (10th ed.). Geneva: Author.

Young, A. R., Beitchman, J. H., Johnson, C., Douglas, L., Atkinson, L., Escobar, M., … Wilson, B. (2002). Young adult academic outcomes in a longitudinal sample of early identified language impaired and control children. *Journal of Child Psychology and Psychiatry, 43*(5), 635–645.

Zahn-Waxler, C. (1993). Warriors and worriers: Gender and psychopathology. *Development and Psychopathology, 5*(1-2), 79–89.

Zenz, T., & Langelett, G. (2004). Special education in Wisconsin's juvenile detention system. *Journal of Correctional Education, 55*(1), 60–68.

Zhang, X., & Tomblin, J.B. (2000). The association of intervention receipt with speech-language profiles and social-demographic variables. *American Journal of Speech-Language Pathology, 9*(4), 345–357.

Zimmerman, I. L., Steiner, V. G., & Pond, R. E. (2011). *PLS-5: Preschool Language Scales* (5th ed.). San Antonio, TX: Pearson.

Zubrick, S. R., Taylor, C. L., Rice, M. L., & Slegers, D. W. (2007). Late language emergence at 24 months: An epidemiological study of prevalence, predictors, and covariates. *Journal of Speech, Language, and Hearing Research, 50*(6), 1562–1592.

Zwi, M., Jones, H., Thorgaard, C., York, A., & Dennis, J. A. (2011). Parent training interventions for attention deficit hyperactivity disorder (ADHD) in children aged 5 to 18 years. *Cochrane Database of Systematic Reviews, 12*. Retrieved from http://www.ncbi.nlm.nih.gov/pubmed/22161373

7

Appendix: Tools and Resources

Appendix 1
Parent Report Guideline for Anxiety Symptoms

For each item check the appropriate box and discuss with your clinician. It is common for children to show some of the symptoms described below without necessarily needing any specific treatment or help with their anxiety. Your clinician can help determine whether the number of symptoms or the severity of the symptoms is such that he/she merits an evaluation for treatment.

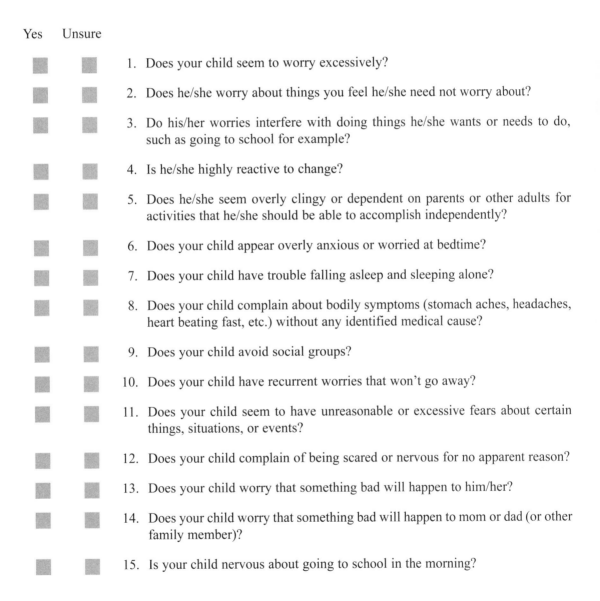

Yes   Unsure

1. Does your child seem to worry excessively?

2. Does he/she worry about things you feel he/she need not worry about?

3. Do his/her worries interfere with doing things he/she wants or needs to do, such as going to school for example?

4. Is he/she highly reactive to change?

5. Does he/she seem overly clingy or dependent on parents or other adults for activities that he/she should be able to accomplish independently?

6. Does your child appear overly anxious or worried at bedtime?

7. Does your child have trouble falling asleep and sleeping alone?

8. Does your child complain about bodily symptoms (stomach aches, headaches, heart beating fast, etc.) without any identified medical cause?

9. Does your child avoid social groups?

10. Does your child have recurrent worries that won't go away?

11. Does your child seem to have unreasonable or excessive fears about certain things, situations, or events?

12. Does your child complain of being scared or nervous for no apparent reason?

13. Does your child worry that something bad will happen to him/her?

14. Does your child worry that something bad will happen to mom or dad (or other family member)?

15. Is your child nervous about going to school in the morning?

Note. This is not a guideline for all forms of anxiety or anxiety disorders, but is restricted to those symptoms of anxiety that are more commonly associated with language impairment.

From: J. Beitchman and E. B. Brownlie: *Language Disorders in Children and Adolescents*   © 2014 Hogrefe Publishing

Appendix 2
Parent and Teacher Report Form for Symptoms of Attention Deficit Hyperactivity

Name: _____ Gender: _____

Age: _____ Grade: _____ Completed by: _____

This form can be used to help identify symptoms associated with attention deficit hyperactivity. It can be filled out by parents and teachers. Return the completed form to your clinician, who will review the responses with you.

For each item, check the column which best describes the child:

	Never	Hardly Ever	Sometimes	Often
1. Fails to give close attention to details or makes careless mistakes in schoolwork or tasks.				
2. Has difficulty sustaining attention in tasks or play activities.				
3. Does not seem to listen when spoken to directly.				
4. Does not follow through on instructions and fails to finish schoolwork, chores, or duties.				
5. Has difficulty organizing tasks and activities.				
6. Avoids or reluctantly engages in tasks requiring sustained mental effort.				
7. Loses things necessary for activities (e.g., toys, school assignments, pencils, or books).				
8. Is easily distracted by extraneous stimuli.				
9. Is forgetful in daily activities.				
10. Has difficulty executing directions.				
11. Fidgets or squirms in seat.				
12. Leaves seat in classroom or in other situations in which remaining seated is expected.				
13. Runs about or climbs excessively in situations in which it is inappropriate.				
14. Has difficulty playing or engaging in leisure activities quietly.				
15. Is "on the go" or acts as if "driven by a motor."				
16. Talks excessively.				
17. Blurts out answers before questions have been completed.				
18. Has difficulty awaiting his/her turn.				

Note. We based the items in this questionnaire on the symptoms associated with attention deficit hyperactivity.

From: J. Beitchman and E. B. Brownlie: *Language Disorders in Children and Adolescents*   © 2014 Hogrefe Publishing

Appendix 3
Parent and Teacher Report Form for Conduct Problems

Name: _____   Gender: _____

Age: _____   Grade: _____   Completed by: _____

This form can be used to help identify symptoms associated with conduct problems. It can be filled out by parents and teachers. Return the completed form to your clinician who will review the responses with you.

For each item, check the column which best describes the child/adolescent:

	Never	Hardly Ever	Some-times	Often	Don't know
1. Bullies, threatens, or intimidates others.					
2. Initiates physical fights.					
3. Has used a weapon that can cause serious physical harm to others (e.g., bat, brick, broken bottle, knife, gun).					
4. Has been physically cruel to people.					
5. Has been physically cruel to animals.					
6. Has stolen while confronting a victim.					
7. Has forced someone into sexual activity.					
8. Has deliberately engaged in fire setting.					
9. Has deliberately destroyed others' property (other than by fire setting).					
10. Has broken into someone else's house, building, or car.					
11. Lies to obtain goods or favors or to avoid obligations.					
12. Has stolen items without confronting a victim (e.g., shoplifting, but without breaking and entering, forgery).					
13. Is truant from school.					
14. Stays out at night despite parental prohibitions.					
15a. Has run away from home overnight at least twice while living in parental or parental surrogate home.					
15b. Has run away from home overnight without returning for a lengthy period.					

Note. We based the items in this questionnaire on the symptoms associated with conduct problems.

From: J. Beitchman and E. B. Brownlie: *Language Disorders in Children and Adolescents*   © 2014 Hogrefe Publishing

Appendix 4
Parent and Teacher Report Form for Oppositional Behavior

Name: _____ Gender: _____

Age: _____ Grade: _____ Completed by: _____

This form can be used to help identify symptoms associated with oppositional behavior. It can be filled out by parents and teachers. Return the completed form to your clinician who will review the responses with you.

For each item, check the column which best describes the child:

	Never	Hardly Ever	Some-times	Often	Don't know
1. Loses temper.					
2. Argues with adults.					
3. Actively defies adults' requests or rules.					
4. Deliberately annoys people.					
5. Blames others for his or her mistakes or misbehavior.					
6. Is touchy or easily annoyed by others.					
7. Is angry and resentful.					
8. Is spiteful or vindictive.					

Note. We based the items in this questionnaire on the symptoms associated with oppositional behavior.

Appendix 5
Handout for Parents: Information on Language Impairment or Delay

What is language impairment?

Language impairment refers to significant difficulties with verbal (spoken) communication. The difficulties can involve expressive language (speaking), receptive language (listening and understanding) or both.

Language impairment may not always be obvious. Compared to others their own age, children with language impairment may:
- develop language more slowly
- use nonspecific words or the wrong word for familiar things
- make more grammatical errors
- have trouble organizing their ideas when speaking or telling stories
- have difficulty understanding what is said to them

What kinds of challenges can children and youth with language issues face?

Below are some difficulties that can come up for some children and youth with language impairment or delay. Not all children have problems in all of these areas.

Communication
- Language difficulties make it more difficult for children and youths to express themselves and understand others.
- Telling stories or explaining what happened may be more difficult.
- Understanding verbal instructions may be more difficult.
- Interacting with peers may be more difficult.

School
- Reading problems are very common.
- Other academic difficulties are also common.
- Motor coordination is sometimes affected.
- Behavior problems can occur if the child or youth doesn't understand what is expected or gets frustrated by their language challenges.

Making friends and getting along with others
- Young children may have trouble joining in at playtime.
- Older children and youths may have trouble interacting in groups or with friendships.

Emotional and behavioural issues
- Children with language impairment can experience high levels of anxiety (fear and worrying).
- Attention problems are also common for children with language impairment.
- Behavior problems can develop, possibly due to school and/or social difficulties, especially among older male youths.

Additional
- Girls with language difficulties may be at increased risk of experiencing sexual abuse before the age of 18.
- Boys with language impairment have a somewhat greater risk of being arrested in adolescence than boys with typical language.

From: J. Beitchman and E. B. Brownlie: *Language Disorders in Children and Adolescents*   © 2014 Hogrefe Publishing

What are the long term outcomes of language impairment?

- Children with language impairment may continue to have more difficulty than their peers with communication and comprehension. However, their language skills continue to develop and improve with age.
- Emotional or behavior problems are common from childhood through late adolescence. These may be related to social difficulties and academic difficulties that arise because of language problems.
- Evidence suggests that emotional/behavioural issues often improve by early adulthood.

What can parents do to help?

Provide encouragement and support
- Recognize the challenges that language difficulties may pose in many aspects of your child's life.
- Notice and encourage your child's strengths. Provide opportunities for your child to develop interests that are not language-focused, such as sports or arts.
- Understand that your child's behavior problems can result from their poor comprehension and frustration related to language difficulties, rather than poor attitude or willful disobedience.

Promote understanding and learning
- Simplify your language and speak slowly so you are easier to understand.
- Check whether your child has understood, especially with new situations. Make sure they understand your expectations for their behavior.
- Break down requests into fewer components.
- Read to your child and encourage them to read materials they find engaging.

Nurture the parent–child relationship
- Find enjoyable activities you can do together.
- Remember to consider your child's perspective and how they may be feeling.
- Prioritize issues to address with your child and avoid being overly critical.
- Be flexible with your expectations for your youth's educational or career choices.

Advocate for your child or youth
- Arrange for services if needed.
- Speak positively about your child to others.
- Understand that language difficulties are not always visible to others and that your child's or youth's behavior may be misinterpreted.
- Communicate with your child's teacher if problems emerge and provide or arrange for extra help if needed.
- Educate your child about sexual abuse and make sure they know they can come to you if they experience uncomfortable or frightening situations.

Appendix 6
Handout for Parents: Online Sources for Information on Language Impairment or Delay

1. **The American Speech-Language-Hearing Association**
   http://www.asha.org/public/
   This site includes a number of resources including information on speech and language development. Language and speech disorders are discussed at
   http://www.asha.org/public/speech/disorders/childsandl.htm

2. **The Canadian Association of Speech-Language Pathologists and Audiologists** has information for the public on speech/language development including resources for preschool children.
   http://www.speechandhearing.ca/

3. **Parentbooks** offers a list of books for parents about speech and language disorders as well as resources for teachers and speech/language therapists:
   http://www.parentbooks.ca/Speech_&_Language_Disorders.html

4. **LD Online** has a section on language impairment for parents.
   http://www.ldonline.org/spearswerling/Specific_Language_Impairment

5. **University of Michigan Health Systems** hosts a website with information on language and speech impairment and tips for parents for encouraging their children's language development and supporting children who stutter.
   http://www.med.umich.edu/yourchild/topics/speech.htm

6. **The National Dissemination Center for Children with Disabilities** has information and resources including tips for parents and teachers of children with language impairment.
   http://nichcy.org/disability/specific/speechlanguage

7. **Talking Point** is a UK-based site with information about children's speech and language development and concerns, and includes resources for parents and professionals (early childhood educators, teachers, family physicians, public health professionals, and speech-language pathologists).
   http://www.talkingpoint.org.uk/Parent.aspx
   The following section of the Talking Point site is aimed at youth.
   http://www.talkingpoint.org.uk/Young-people.aspx

8. **The Encyclopedia of Language and Literacy Development** is a science-based online resource aimed at educators, which includes a section on speech and language disorders.
   http://literacyencyclopedia.ca/

From: J. Beitchman and E. B. Brownlie: *Language Disorders in Children and Adolescents*   © 2014 Hogrefe Publishing

Appendix 7
Handout for Parents: Practicing Emotions With Your Child

Here is a list of emotion words and some examples of situations in which a child would experience these feelings. Use every-day situations to illustrate feelings. Help your child by showing the facial expression that corresponds to the feeling you believe appropriate for the situation. Be sure to use examples reflective of the child's experiences.

You can make a separate page for each feeling and review these feelings with your child. Be sure to show the child the facial expression and ask the child to make the facial expression of that feeling. Then talk about the feeling with the child explaining that the feelings are normal for the particular situation. Encourage the child to use words to express the feeling being discussed and to try to do so at the time of the relevant event. Model some of the emotion words to assist your child if he/she has trouble doing so.

1. Things that make me feel **HAPPY**:

   a. Being with mommy or daddy
   b. Playing with my favorite toy or game

2. Things that make me feel **MAD**:

   a. When (sibling, anyone) takes my toys or my things
   b. When I can't do something, I really want to do

3. Things that make me feel **SCARED**:

   a. When it is dark and I hear funny noises
   b. When I have to go to school

4. Things that make me feel **WORRIED**:

   a. When mommy or daddy go away
   b. When I have to read out loud in school

5. Things that make me feel **RELAXED** or **CALM**:

   a. When I have free time to do what I like
   b. When my mother reads me a story

6. Things that make me feel **SAD**:

   a. When I lose in a game
   b. When no one wants to play with me

From: J. Beitchman and E. B. Brownlie: *Language Disorders in Children and Adolescents*   © 2014 Hogrefe Publishing

7. Things that make me feel **EMBARRASSED**:

   a. When I make a mistake in front of the class
   b. When kids laugh at my clothes

8. Things that make me **TENSE** or **NERVOUS**:

   a. When I am sent down to see the principal
   b. When mommy or daddy are very late coming home

9. Things that make me feel **PROUD**:

   a. When I learn to do something new
   b. When my friends say I did good

10. Things that make me feel **EXCITED**:

   a. When I am getting presents
   a. When I can play with my friends

From: J. Beitchman and E. B. Brownlie: *Language Disorders in Children and Adolescents*   © 2014 Hogrefe Publishing

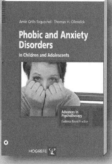